Better Homes and Gardens®

FIX & FREEZE

COOK BOOK

Our seal assures you that every recipe in the
Fix & Freeze Cook Book
has been tested in the Better Homes and Gardens® Test Kitchen.
This means that each recipe is practical and
reliable, and meets our high standards of taste appeal.

BETTER HOMES AND GARDENS® BOOKS

Editor: Gerald M. Knox
Art Director: Ernest Shelton
Managing Editor: David A. Kirchner
Copy and Production Editors: James D. Blume, Marsha Jahns,
   Rosanne Weber Mattson, Mary Helen Schiltz

Food and Nutrition Editor: Nancy Byal
Department Head, Cook Books: Sharyl Heiken
Associate Department Heads: Sandra Granseth,
   Rosemary C. Hutchinson, Elizabeth Woolever
Senior Food Editors: Julia Malloy, Marcia Stanley, Joyce Trollope
Associate Food Editors: Barbara Atkins, Linda Henry,
   Mary Jo Plutt, Maureen Powers, Martha Schiel,
   Linda Foley Woodrum
Recipe Development Editor: Marion Viall
Test Kitchen Director: Sharon Stilwell
Test Kitchen Photo Studio Director: Janet Pittman
Test Kitchen Home Economists: Jean Brekke, Kay Cargill,
   Marilyn Cornelius, Jennifer Darling, Maryellyn Krantz,
   Lynelle Munn, Dianna Nolin, Marge Steenson, Cynthia Volcko

Associate Art Directors: Linda Ford Vermie, Neoma Alt West,
   Randall Yontz
Assistant Art Directors: Lynda Haupert, Harijs Priekulis,
   Tom Wegner
Senior Graphic Designers: Jack Murphy, Stan Sams,
   Darla Whipple-Frain
Graphic Designers: Mike Burns, Sally Cooper,
   Brian Wignall, Kimberly Zarley

Vice President, Editorial Director: Doris Eby
Executive Director, Editorial Services: Duane L. Gregg

Senior Vice President, General Manager: Fred Stines
Director of Publishing: Robert B. Nelson
Vice President, Retail Marketing: Jamie Martin
Vice President, Direct Marketing: Arthur Heydendael

FIX & FREEZE COOK BOOK

Editor: Linda Foley Woodrum
Copy and Production Editor: James D. Blume
Graphic Designer: Sally Cooper
Electronic Text Processor: Joyce Wasson
Contributing Photographers: Ron Crofoot, Scott Little
Food Stylists: Janet Pittman, Maria Rolandelli

On the front cover: Paella-Style Chicken
(see recipe, page 25)

Fix and freeze...believe me, it's as simple as it sounds! I have lots of ideas to help you fix recipes, freeze them, then enjoy them later. Which foods freeze better than others? How should you package foods for the freezer? How do you reheat the food once it's frozen? The answers are all here, and much more.

The single-serving entrées in the first chapter were particularly challenging to develop. Trying to duplicate individual frozen dinners from the supermarket was harder than I thought it would be. But with the help of the Test Kitchen, I was able to come up with a chapter full of winning recipes.

And if it's family-size recipes you need, don't worry. There are also chapters brimming with delicious recipes for 2 to 12 servings. Like me, you may have a hard time resisting the recipe for Paella-Style Chicken on page 25 or the French Onion Soup on page 43.

So move over ice cubes, you've got company! By using this book, you can keep your freezer stocked with homemade goodies that are ready to reheat and enjoy—anytime.

Linda J. Woodrum

Foolproof Freezing

Freezing is one of nature's simplest and best ways to preserve food. So take full advantage of it! You can prepare a meal days or even months ahead and freeze it. Then just take it out of the freezer and pop it into the oven. You'll be able to enjoy a marvelous meal at a moment's notice. As with any kind of food preparation, though, freezing requires certain precautions.

Wrap It Up
The term "freezer burn" may sound contradictory, but it describes well what happens to food when it is exposed to extreme cold. Food exposed to the freezer's cold air discolors and usually dries out on the surface. Proper wrapping will prevent this. A good wrapping material has these characteristics:
- moisture- and vaporproof
- durable
- resistant to oil and grease
- easy to label.

The following wrapping materials all meet those criteria:
Aluminum Foil. Heavy-duty foil provides better protection for food in the freezer than regular foil. Mold the foil to the shape of the food to keep air out. Just be sure the foil doesn't puncture while you're wrapping the food.

A word of caution: Don't use foil to wrap foods that contain acid, such as tomato products. Acid reacts with the aluminum, giving the

food an off-flavor. If foil is the only freezer wrap you have on hand, wrap the food first in clear plastic wrap, then overwrap with foil.
Laminated Wrap. Sturdy laminated paper, also known as heavy freezer paper.
Freezer Plastic Wrap. This clear plastic material is sturdier than everyday plastic wrap. Because not all plastic wraps are alike, read the label to make sure your wrap is freezer-safe.

Credible Containers
Packaging food in proper freezer containers is another good way to freeze food. Here's a list of containers that can withstand cold temperatures:
Aluminum Containers. These are available in many sizes and styles with tight-fitting lids. Many are reusable and can go from freezer to oven and back again.
Baking Dishes. Use dishes that are recommended for freezer-to-oven and/or freezer-to-microwave oven.
Polyethylene Bags. These bags are made from pliable plastic film and are moisture- and vaporproof. The bags work well for solid foods, but

they don't store easily when filled with liquids. Polyethylene bags come in various sizes and shapes. Some bags come with boxes, which add protection as well as help shape the bag for easy stacking.

Boil-in-the-Bag Containers. These pouches made of polyester film can withstand temperature changes from below 0° F to 240° when reheated. You will need a special heat-sealing device to seal the bags before freezing. Reheat the frozen food by immersing the unopened bag in boiling water. For more specifics, follow the manufacturer's instructions.

Plastic Cartons. These containers come in a variety of sizes with tight-fitting lids.

Waxed Cartons. Reusable waxed cardboard containers come in a variety of shapes and sizes. If you intend to pack them with foods that stain, line them first with polyethylene bags.

Metal Boxes or Cans. These are good for cookies or delicate foods that are easily smashed. Separate the layers of food with waxed paper and seal the lid with freezer tape.

Glass Freezing Jars. These include pint and quart jars that are tempered for temperature extremes. The jars have slightly tapered sides and wide mouths. The conventional canning jar may be used for freezing, but because its mouth is narrow,

food must be thawed before it is removed.

Plastic-Treated Paper Plates, Cups, and Bowls. These containers are safe to use for short-term storage. If you plan to store food in them for longer than one month, overwrap with freezer plastic wrap or heavy-duty foil.

Freezer-Safe Sealing
Sealing food correctly is just as important as the wrap or container it's frozen in.

Liquid or semi-liquid foods, such as soups and stews, will expand when they freeze so leave about ½ inch of space below the rim (headspace). All other foods should be sealed with as little air in the container as possible.

Once the food is wrapped, seal packages and loose-

fitting lids with freezer tape. You can buy freezer tape at your supermarket. It may look the same as masking tape, but freezer tape sticks better in cold temperatures.

Versatile Packaging
Freezing food in a casserole or dish doesn't mean the container has to be stranded in the freezer till you're ready to reheat the food. Simply line the dish with heavy-duty foil three times the width or diameter of the dish. Center the foil, add the food, and cool. Bring the longer sides of the foil together over the food. Fold down the foil, pressing air out, until the foil is folded down next to the food. Fold down the shorter sides of the foil. Freeze until firm. Then lift the foil-

Recipe Pointers
● Look before you leap! Many recipes contain ingredients that aren't needed until serving time. For instance, don't bake the patty shells for Shrimp-Swiss Patty Shells until you reheat the frozen mixture (see recipe, page 28). So read through each recipe before starting.
● During recipe testing, we froze most mixtures in freezer containers. If you use freezer bags, the frozen mixture may not be as deep as a frozen block

of food from a container. Therefore, the reheating time may be shorter.
● Calorie counters take note. Some recipes list the number of calories per serving near the title. These recipes are calorie-reduced and are scattered throughout the book.
● You've made a recipe and can't wait to eat some. No problem! Just remember that if you're heating only a portion of the food, the timing may be shorter.

wrapped food from the dish and store the food in the freezer. When you're ready to reheat, unwrap the frozen food and return it to the original dish. You'll get an exact fit every time!

Packaging Pitfalls

Unfortunately, not all wraps and containers are freezer-safe. The following products are *not* moisture- and vaporproof, so *don't* freeze food in them:

Wraps. Aluminum foil other than heavy-duty, waxed paper, and plastic wraps not labeled for freezer use.

Rigid Containers. Glass jars not recommended for freezing (such as mayonnaise jars), pottery, nonflexible plastic, Styrofoam, and untreated cardboard containers.

Plastic Bags. Any bags not labeled as freezer bags.

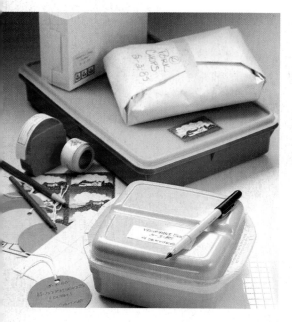

Letter-Perfect Labeling

Have you ever peered into your freezer and found unmarked mystery packages of food staring back at you? Avoid this by properly labeling foods. Labeling also clues you in to which packages are the oldest and should be used first.

When labeling your package, include the following information:
- type of food
- quantity, weight, or number of servings
- date frozen
- any specific information about future use.

For the recipes in this book, you may want to jot the reheating instructions on the package if there's room. Then you won't have to look up the recipe to get the reheating time when you pull the food from the freezer.

You can label packages with a wax crayon, ballpoint pen, waterproof marking pen, or pencil. Write directly on the package or use adhesive or tie-on labels.

Attention, Microwave Owners

The power of microwave ovens varies, so check the wattage of your oven in the owner's manual. For the microwave reheating charts in this book, we used 600- to 700-watt ovens. If your oven differs, use your owner's manual as a guide.

The Cold Facts

Freezing foods is easy. Here's a quick checklist for successful freezing:

1. Set your freezer temperature at 0° F or below to maintain the best food color, flavor, and texture. A freezer thermometer will help you keep a check on the temperature.

2. Use proper moisture- and vaporproof wrap and containers for freezing. Seal the packages securely to prevent freezer burn.

3. Quickly cool hot foods before freezing.

4. When you add food to the freezer, separate the packages until they are solidly frozen. This allows the cold air to circulate around the packages.

5. Label and date each package you place in the freezer.

6. Limit how much food you freeze at one time. Freeze only two to three pounds of food per cubic foot of total storage space within a 24-hour period.

7. Follow the recommended freezer storage times. You'll find these listed near the beginning of each chapter.

SINGLE-SERVING ENTRÉES

No matter whether you're living alone or a member of a busy family, this section was written with your needs in mind. We show you how to divide a selection of recipes into individual servings and freeze them. For a last-minute meal, just grab one from the freezer, follow our reheating directions, and voilà! A hassle-free single-serving meal. And guess what? No leftovers!

Oven Reheating Tips

When there's more than one hungry person ready to eat, go ahead and pop as many single-serving entrées into the oven as you like. The reheating time we give in the recipe for one serving will work fine for more than one, too.

If you're planning to reheat one serving and own a toaster oven, use it instead of a conventional oven. Single servings reheated in a toaster oven use less energy and take about the same amount of time as in a conventional oven.

Divide and Conquer

If you're used to buying for one or a few, take advantage of special prices on larger portions. Next time whole chickens are on sale, buy one. You can cut it up, wrap the pieces in six serving-size portions, and freeze them. The same goes for whole chicken breasts. One breast is enough for two servings, so halve the breasts lengthwise. Freeze each half-breast serving separately so it's ready when you are.

Go ahead and buy that pound of ground meat, too. For quick burgers from the freezer, shape the meat into four patties and freeze them. To easily separate the burgers, stack them with two layers of waxed paper between each patty before freezing.

And make the most of those succulent roasts. Slice a large roast into smaller servings and freeze them, either as whole pieces or as slices to use for a stir-fry.

How Long Will It Keep?

A frozen food will keep for a long time, but not forever. Food that is kept in the freezer for too long suffers in flavor and texture. As a general guide, you can store the recipes in this chapter for three to six months.

Shrimp Creole

229 CALORIES / SERVING

This tongue-tingling seafood dish has been a favorite of many Louisiana folks for years.

Nonstick spray coating
1 medium onion, chopped
½ cup chopped celery
¼ cup chopped green pepper
2 cloves garlic, minced
1 16-ounce can tomatoes,
    cut up
2 tablespoons snipped parsley
⅛ to ¼ teaspoon ground red
    pepper
1 bay leaf
2 tablespoons cornstarch
2 tablespoons cold water
1 12-ounce package frozen
    shelled shrimp
2 tablespoons tomato paste
¼ cup quick-cooking rice

● Spray a 10-inch skillet with nonstick coating. Cook onion, celery, green pepper, and garlic in the skillet till onion is tender but not brown. Stir in *undrained* tomatoes, parsley, red pepper, and bay leaf.

● Bring to boiling; reduce heat. Cover and simmer for 15 minutes. Stir together cornstarch and water. Add to skillet. Cook and stir till thickened and bubbly, then cook and stir 2 minutes more. (Mixture will be thick.) Remove from the heat. Discard bay leaf. Stir in frozen shrimp and tomato paste. Spoon into 4 individual freezer containers. Seal, label, and freeze.

● **To serve,** in a small saucepan cook 1 portion of frozen mixture, covered, in a small saucepan over medium-low heat for 10 to 15 minutes or till heated through and shrimp are tender, stirring occasionally. Meanwhile, prepare rice according to package directions. Spoon shrimp mixture over rice. Makes 4 single-serving entrées.

Baked Fish with Bulgur Pilaf

273 CALORIES / SERVING

Bulgur (precooked cracked wheat) takes the place of rice.

1 pound fresh *or* frozen
    halibut steaks, cut 1 inch
    thick
¾ cup sliced fresh mushrooms
⅓ cup chopped onion
⅓ cup sliced celery
1 teaspoon cooking oil
½ cup water
⅓ cup bulgur wheat
¼ cup snipped dried apricots
½ teaspoon instant chicken
    bouillon granules
⅓ cup shredded carrot
Butter *or* margarine

● Partially thaw fish steaks, if frozen. Cut fish into 4 serving-size pieces. Season lightly with salt and pepper.

● In a small saucepan cook mushrooms, onion, and celery in hot oil for 1 minute. Stir in water, bulgur, apricots, and bouillon granules. Bring to boiling; remove from the heat. Stir in carrot; cool. Spoon bulgur mixture into 4 individual casseroles. Place fish portions on top of bulgur mixture. Seal, label, and freeze.

● **To serve,** bake 1 frozen casserole, covered, in a 375° oven for 60 to 70 minutes or till heated through. Melt some butter; brush it lightly over fish. Makes 4 single-serving entrées.

Chicken Florentine with
Baby Carrots

Chicken Florentine with Baby Carrots

2 whole medium chicken
  breasts, skinned, boned,
  and halved lengthwise
  Salt and pepper
2 tablespoons cooking oil
½ cup chopped onion
2 cloves garlic, minced
2 teaspoons cornstarch
1¼ cups milk
½ of a 3-ounce package cream
  cheese, cut up
2 tablespoons dry white wine
1 pound fresh spinach,
  stems removed
8 ounces fresh baby carrots *or*
  4 medium carrots, bias-
  sliced into 1-inch pieces

● Sprinkle chicken with salt and pepper. In a large skillet brown chicken in hot oil about 12 minutes or just till tender, turning once. Remove from skillet, reserving drippings. For sauce, cook onion and garlic in reserved drippings till tender. Stir in cornstarch. Add milk all at once. Cook and stir till thickened and bubbly; cook and stir for 2 minutes more. Stir in cheese till it melts. Remove from heat. Stir in wine.

● Rinse spinach in water. In a large saucepan cook spinach, covered, in just the water that clings to the leaves. Reduce the heat when steam forms, then cook, covered, about 3 minutes or till spinach is tender. Drain well; squeeze out excess liquid. Cook carrots in a small amount of boiling water for 2 to 3 minutes or till crisp-tender; drain.

● Arrange cooked spinach in 4 individual casseroles. Place chicken on spinach; pour sauce over the chicken. Add carrots. Seal, label, and freeze.

● **To serve,** bake 1 frozen casserole, loosely covered, in a 375° oven for 50 to 60 minutes or till heated through. Sprinkle with paprika and garnish with small spinach leaves, if desired. Makes 4 single-serving entrées.

Cashew Chicken

¼ cup soy sauce
¼ cup dry sherry
1 tablespoon quick-cooking
  tapioca, ground (see tip,
  page 14)
1 teaspoon sugar
½ teaspoon grated gingerroot
¼ teaspoon crushed red
  pepper
1 tablespoon cooking oil
2 medium carrots, thinly bias
  sliced
1 medium green pepper, cut
  into ¾-inch pieces
1 small onion, cut into wedges
2 whole medium chicken
  breasts, skinned, boned,
  and cut into 1-inch pieces
  Cashews

● For sauce, stir together soy sauce, sherry, tapioca, sugar, gingerroot, pepper, and ⅔ cup *water*. Set aside. Preheat a wok or large skillet over high heat; add oil. (Add more oil as necessary during cooking.) Stir-fry carrots, green pepper, and onion in hot oil for 2 minutes. Remove from wok.

● Add *half* of the chicken to the hot wok. Stir-fry for 2 minutes. Remove from wok. Stir-fry remaining chicken for 2 minutes. Return all chicken to wok. Push chicken from center of wok. Stir sauce; add to wok. Cook and stir till bubbly; cook and stir for 2 minutes more. Remove from the heat. Stir in vegetables; cool. Spoon into 4 individual casseroles. Seal, label, and freeze.

● **To serve,** bake 1 frozen casserole, covered, in a 375° oven for 35 to 40 minutes or till heated through. Or place one portion of the frozen mixture in a small saucepan. Cover and cook over medium-low heat for 15 to 20 minutes or till heated through, stirring occasionally. Sprinkle with cashews. Makes 4 single-serving entrées.

Grinding Tapioca

Kiss those lumps good-bye! Unlike flour and cornstarch, tapioca retains its thickness when frozen and reheated. Unfortunately it retains its characteristic lumps, too. An easy way to smooth out sauces thickened with tapioca is to grind the dry tapioca in a blender or food processor.

Simply place ¼ cup of quick-cooking *tapioca* in a blender container or food processor bowl. Cover and blend till the tapioca resembles coarse salt. Then store the tapioca in a cool dry place and use it whenever a recipe in the book calls for quick-cooking tapioca, ground.

Turkey-Stuffed Manicotti

Turkey sausage really boosts the flavor of the filling.

4 manicotti shells
1 8-ounce can tomato sauce
1 7½-ounce can tomatoes, cut up
¼ cup dry red wine
1 tablespoon quick-cooking tapioca, ground (see tip, above)
½ teaspoon dried basil, crushed
½ teaspoon dried oregano, crushed
8 ounces ground turkey sausage
¼ cup chopped onion
1 clove garlic, minced
½ of a 10-ounce package frozen chopped broccoli, thawed and well drained
½ cup shredded mozzarella cheese (2 ounces)
2 tablespoons grated Parmesan cheese
Grated Parmesan cheese

● Cook manicotti according to package directions; drain. Rinse with cold water; drain. Set aside.

● For sauce, in a small saucepan stir together tomato sauce, *undrained* tomatoes, wine, tapioca, basil, and oregano. Cook and stir till thickened and bubbly, then cook and stir for 2 minutes more. Set aside.

● In a medium skillet cook turkey sausage, onion, and garlic till meat is brown and onion is tender. Drain off fat, if necessary. Stir in broccoli, mozzarella cheese, and 2 tablespoons Parmesan cheese. Stir in *⅓ cup* of the sauce; cool.

● Spoon *2 tablespoons* of the sauce into the bottom of *each* of 4 individual casseroles. Spoon about *⅓ cup* meat mixture into *each* manicotti. Place stuffed manicotti in casseroles. Spoon any remaining meat mixture around shells. Pour remaining sauce over manicotti, completely covering pasta so it doesn't dry out during reheating. Seal, label, and freeze.

● **To serve,** bake 1 frozen casserole, covered, in a 375° oven about 60 minutes or till heated through. Sprinkle with additional Parmesan cheese. Makes 4 single-serving entrées.

Turkey Lasagna

254 CALORIES SERVING

Look for ground raw turkey in your grocer's freezer.

4 lasagna noodles
1 pound ground raw turkey
¼ cup chopped onion
1 clove garlic, minced
1 7½-ounce can tomatoes
1 15-ounce can tomato sauce
½ teaspoon dried basil, crushed
¼ teaspoon dried oregano, crushed
1 4-ounce can mushroom stems and pieces, drained
1 cup ricotta cheese (part skim milk)
2 tablespoons snipped parsley
2 tablespoons grated Parmesan cheese
2 tablespoons skim milk
¾ cup shredded mozzarella cheese (part skim milk)

● Cook noodles according to package directions; drain. Meanwhile, in a large skillet cook turkey, onion, and garlic till meat is brown and onion is tender. Drain off fat, if necessary. Cut up the tomatoes. Stir *undrained* tomatoes, tomato sauce, basil, and oregano into turkey mixture. Bring to boiling; reduce the heat. Simmer, uncovered, for 10 minutes. Stir in mushrooms. Stir together ricotta, parsley, Parmesan, milk, and ⅛ teaspoon *pepper.*

● Arrange *half* of the noodles in the bottom of a 10x6x2-inch baking dish, trimming to fit. Spread with *half* of the meat mixture. Layer remaining noodles, all of the ricotta mixture, and remaining meat mixture. Sprinkle with mozzarella.

● Cover dish; freeze for 1½ to 2 hours or till nearly firm. Remove from the freezer. Cut into 6 portions. Transfer each piece to a lightly greased individual casserole. Seal, label, and freeze.

● **To serve,** bake 1 frozen casserole, covered, in a 375° oven for 50 minutes. Uncover; bake about 10 minutes more or till heated through. Let stand 5 minutes. Makes 6 single-serving entrées.

Dividing lasagna into single-serving portions
After assembling the lasagna, cover the dish and freeze it for 1½ to 2 hours or till nearly firm. This partially freezes the lasagna, making it easier to cut and remove the portions. Use a wide spatula to transfer each serving to an individual casserole.

Scrambled Eggs Deluxe

This complete breakfast bakes while you're getting ready to go.

3 frozen hash brown potato
   patties
2 tablespoons butter *or*
   margarine
¼ cup sliced green onion
6 beaten eggs
¼ cup milk
1 single-serving envelope
   instant cream of chicken
   soup mix
1 4-ounce can sliced
   mushrooms, drained
2 tablespoons chopped
   pimiento
⅛ teaspoon pepper
4 ounces fully cooked
   smoked *or* brown-and-
   serve sausage, sliced

● In a large skillet cook potato patties in *1 tablespoon* of the butter or margarine on 1 side only for 2 to 3 minutes or till light brown. Remove from the skillet.

● In the same skillet cook onion in remaining butter or margarine till tender. In a medium mixing bowl combine eggs, milk, and soup mix; beat with a rotary beater till well combined. Stir in mushrooms, pimiento, and pepper. Add to onion in skillet.

● Cook, without stirring, over medium heat till eggs are nearly set, lifting and folding partially cooked eggs so uncooked portion flows underneath. Remove from the heat while eggs are still very moist. Cool slightly.

● Spoon the egg mixture into 3 greased individual casseroles. Arrange sausage and potato patties, browned side up, in casseroles. Seal with foil, label, and freeze.

● **To serve,** turn back foil on 1 frozen casserole to uncover potato patty only. Bake in a 375° oven for 35 to 40 minutes or till hot. Makes 3 single-serving breakfast entrées.

Orange French Toast

Friends joining you for breakfast? Prepare the entire batch by baking the frozen slices of toast on a large baking sheet.

3 eggs
1½ cups orange juice
2 tablespoons brown sugar
12 slices French bread, cut
   ¾ inch thick
1 tablespoon butter *or*
   margarine
2 slices bacon
   Maple-flavored syrup

● In a small bowl combine eggs, juice, and sugar. Beat with a rotary beater till well combined. For easier dipping, transfer the mixture to a 9-inch pie plate. Dip bread into egg mixture, turning to coat both sides. Let bread stand in egg mixture about 30 seconds per side or till thoroughly soaked. Place bread on a baking sheet lined with waxed paper; freeze about 1 hour or till firm. Transfer to freezer bags; seal, label, and freeze.

● **To serve,** place 2 slices of frozen bread in a well-buttered shallow casserole or on a baking sheet. Melt butter or margarine; drizzle over bread. Bake in a 500° oven for 5 minutes. Turn and bake about 3 minutes more or till golden brown.

● Meanwhile, in a small skillet cook bacon till crisp; drain on paper towels. Arrange French toast and bacon on a plate. Pour syrup over toast. Makes 6 single-serving breakfast entrées.

Scrambled Eggs Deluxe

Peppery Wild Rice-Stuffed Chops

¼ cup wild rice
¾ cup water
¼ cup dry sherry
1 cup chopped fresh
    mushrooms
¼ cup chopped onion
2 tablespoons butter *or*
    margarine
¼ teaspoon salt
¼ teaspoon ground sage
4 pork loin rib chops, cut 1
    inch thick (about 2¼
    pounds total)
1 to 2 tablespoons coarsely
    crushed black pepper
1 teaspoon paprika
1 cup beef broth
1 tablespoon quick-cooking
    tapioca, ground (see tip,
    page 14)
1 tablespoon dry sherry

● Run cold water over rice in a strainer for 1 minute, lifting rice with fingers. In a small saucepan combine rice, ¾ cup water, and ¼ cup sherry. Bring to boiling; reduce the heat. Cover and simmer about 40 minutes or till rice is just tender. Drain.

● In a medium skillet cook mushrooms and onion in butter or margarine till onion is tender. Remove from the heat; divide mushroom mixture in half. Stir rice mixture, salt, and sage into *half* of the mushroom mixture; cool.

● Make a pocket in each chop by cutting from the fat side almost to bone edge. Spoon about 3 tablespoons rice mixture into each chop. Close the opening with wooden toothpicks.

● Stir together pepper and paprika. Sprinkle over stuffed chops; rub mixture in with your fingers. Place chops on the unheated rack of a broiler pan. Broil 5 inches from the heat for 8 minutes. Turn and broil for 6 to 8 minutes more or till nearly done. Cool slightly; remove toothpicks.

● For sauce, in a small saucepan stir together broth and tapioca. Add remaining mushroom mixture. Cook and stir till thickened and bubbly, then cook and stir for 2 minutes more. Stir in 1 tablespoon sherry. Spoon sauce into 4 individual casseroles. Top with chops. Seal, label, and freeze.

● **To serve,** bake 1 frozen casserole, covered, in a 375° oven for 1 to 1¼ hours or till heated through. Spoon sauce over chops before serving. Makes 4 single-serving entrées.

Stuffing the pork chops
Use a sharp knife to make a pocket in each chop by cutting horizontally from the fat side almost to the bone edge. Then lightly spoon about 3 tablespoons of the rice mixture into each chop. It's easier if you use a small spoon to stuff the chops.

Savory Sauced Short Ribs

8 **beef short ribs**
    (2½ to 3 pounds total)
1 **8-ounce can tomato sauce**
1 **cup beer** *or* **beef broth**
1 **medium onion, chopped**
2 **tablespoons brown sugar**
2 **tablespoons vinegar**
1 **teaspoon Worcestershire**
    sauce
¾ **teaspoon dry mustard**
¼ **teaspoon salt**
⅛ **teaspoon paprika**
1 **tablespoon cornstarch**
1 **tablespoon cold water**
4 **ounces medium noodles**

● Trim excess fat from ribs. In a Dutch oven or large kettle cover ribs with water. Bring to boiling; reduce the heat. Cover and simmer for 1¼ to 1½ hours or till tender. Drain well.

● Meanwhile, for sauce, in a medium saucepan combine tomato sauce, beer or broth, onion, sugar, vinegar, Worcestershire sauce, mustard, salt, and paprika. Bring to boiling; reduce the heat. Cover and simmer for 10 minutes. Stir together cornstarch and cold water; add to sauce. Cook and stir till thickened and bubbly, then cook and stir for 2 minutes more. Remove from the heat; cool.

● Cook noodles in boiling salted water for 4 to 6 minutes or till almost tender; drain. Toss noodles with ⅔ *cup* of the sauce. Arrange noodles in 4 individual casseroles. Place 2 ribs in each casserole. Pour remaining sauce over all. Seal, label, and freeze.

● **To serve,** bake 1 frozen casserole, covered, in a 375° oven for 1 to 1¼ hours or till hot. Makes 4 single-serving entrées.

Stuffed Steak Rolls with Whipped Potatoes

1½ pounds boneless beef round
    steak
3 slices bacon, halved cross-
    wise
1 9-ounce package frozen
    whole green beans,
    thawed
3 small carrots, cut into
    julienne strips
1 10¼-ounce can beef gravy
    Packaged instant mashed
    potatoes (enough for 6
    servings)
¼ cup snipped parsley

● Cut steak into 6 portions; pound to ¼-inch thickness. In a large skillet cook bacon till crisp; remove from skillet, reserving drippings. Place 1 piece of bacon and several green beans and carrot strips on each meat portion. Roll up jelly-roll style. Secure with wooden toothpicks. Brown meat on all sides in hot drippings; drain. Add gravy; cover and simmer about 45 minutes or till meat is tender. Remove picks. Meanwhile, prepare potatoes according to package directions; stir in parsley. Cool.

● Place meat rolls in 6 individual casseroles. Spoon potato mixture in mounds next to meat. Pour gravy over meat and around potatoes. Seal, label, and freeze.

● **To serve,** bake 1 frozen casserole, covered, in a 375° oven for 60 to 70 minutes or till hot. Makes 6 single-serving entrées.

Microwave
Reheating Chart

Use the timings listed at right as a guide for reheating frozen foods in a microwave oven. Apply the timings to similar recipes in this chapter or to your own.
  Here's how the chart works. To reheat a frozen cheesy pasta dish, such as macaroni and cheese, micro-cook 1 cup of the mixture about 8 minutes or 2 cups about 13½ minutes. (To reheat larger portions, see chart on page 31.) All frozen foods were reheated on 70% power (MEDIUM-HIGH), stirring occasionally.

Mixture	1 cup	2 cups
Beef Stroganoff	5 min.	10 min.
Chicken chow mein	7 min.	11 min.
Lobster Newburg	5 min.	11 min.
Macaroni and cheese	8 min.	13½ min.
Roast beef with gravy	11 min.	16 min.
Spaghetti and meat sauce	7 min.	12 min.
Tuna-noodle casserole	5 min.	8 min.

OVEN AND RANGE-TOP DISHES

Look what's ahead in this chapter! You can feast on a variety of down-home family favorites such as saucy Swiss Steak and Lasagna for a Crowd. Or indulge in some of the special-occasion recipes such as the elegant Beef Steaks Wellington. Some of the recipes reheat in the oven—others on top of the range. Either way, you'll find plenty of recipes to suit any taste.

Oven and Range-Top Tips

Cool It!

Before you freeze cooked food, it's important to cool the mixture quickly so bacteria don't grow. The more food you have, the longer it takes to cool.

A slick way to quickly cool large amounts of cooked food is to place the container of warm food in an ice bath. Simply fill your sink or a large bowl with ice. Then wedge the container into the ice and stir the food occasionally. By stirring it, you make sure the center of the food cools, too.

Single-Serving Suggestions

If it's single servings you want, then you can have them! Although this chapter gives recipes and reheating times for four or more servings, you still can package the recipes in individual servings and reheat them one at a time.

Let's look at some examples. You can freeze separate bundles of food individually, such as Stuffed Chicken Rolls on the opposite page, and reheat them one at a time in the oven. Just follow the reheating times in the recipes. Or package saucy mixtures, such as Newburg-Style Lobster on page 28, in individual freezer containers. Reheat a single portion in a small saucepan, but check it sooner than you would the entire amount to see if it's hot.

The only recipe in this section that isn't recommended for single servings is the Vegetarian Quiche on page 35.

How Long Will It Keep?

Do yourself and your frozen food a favor by storing food no longer than the recommended storage times. You can damage the quality of the food by keeping it in the freezer too long. As a general guide, you can store the recipes in this chapter for three to six months.

Stuffed Chicken Rolls

To check for doneness, turn over the coated chicken and cut into the meat to see if it's tender.

4 whole large chicken breasts, skinned, boned, and halved lengthwise
¼ cup chopped onion
1 tablespoon butter *or* margarine
1 6-ounce can crabmeat, drained, flaked, and cartilage removed
1 4-ounce can mushroom stems and pieces, drained and chopped
¼ cup crushed shredded wheat wafers (6 crackers)
2 tablespoons snipped parsley
Dash pepper
4 thin slices Swiss cheese, halved (3 ounces)
1 cup crushed shredded wheat wafers (24 crackers)
2 tablespoons grated Parmesan cheese
1 teaspoon paprika
3 tablespoons milk

● Place 1 chicken piece, boned side up, between 2 pieces of waxed paper. Working from the center to the edges, pound chicken with a meat mallet to about ⅛-inch thickness. Repeat with remaining chicken.

● In a medium skillet cook onion in butter or margarine till tender. Stir in crab, mushrooms, ¼ cup crumbs, parsley, and pepper. Place a halved cheese slice on each chicken piece, trimming, if necessary, to fit within ¼ inch of edges. Spoon about ¼ cup crab mixture onto each chicken piece. Fold in sides of chicken and roll up. Press to seal.

● In a small mixing bowl stir together 1 cup crumbs, Parmesan cheese, and paprika. Brush chicken with milk, then roll it in crumb mixture. Place chicken, seam side down, on a baking sheet. Freeze for 1 hour. Transfer chicken to freezer bags or containers. Seal, label, and freeze.

● **To serve,** place frozen chicken rolls, seam side down, on a rack in a shallow baking pan. Cover and bake in a 375° oven for 1 hour. Uncover and bake for 20 to 30 minutes more or till chicken is heated through. Makes 8 servings.

Tamale Pie

Paella-Style Chicken

Converted rice maintains its firm texture when frozen. (Recipe pictured on the cover.)

2 whole large chicken breasts, skinned, boned, and cut into bite-size pieces
2 tablespoons cooking oil
2 medium onions, quartered
2 medium carrots, cut into julienne strips
½ cup chopped celery
1 14½-ounce can chicken broth
⅔ cup converted long grain rice
1 4-ounce jar diced pimiento, drained
1 clove garlic, minced
¼ teaspoon dried oregano, crushed
¼ teaspoon thread saffron, crushed
1 10-ounce package frozen peas

● In a large skillet cook chicken in hot oil over medium-high heat about 6 minutes or just till tender, stirring frequently. Remove from skillet, reserving oil. Set chicken aside.

● In the skillet cook onions, carrots, and celery over medium heat for 5 minutes. Stir in broth, rice, pimiento, garlic, oregano, and saffron. Bring to boiling; reduce heat. Cover and simmer for 10 minutes. Stir in chicken and peas. Divide mixture in half; cool. Spoon into two 1-quart freezer bags. Seal, label, and freeze.

● **To serve,** transfer 1 portion of the frozen mixture to a large skillet. Add 1 tablespoon *water.* Cover and cook over medium-low heat for 30 to 40 minutes or till heated through, stirring occasionally. Makes two 4-serving portions.

Tamale Pie

285 CALORIES SERVING

The cornmeal topper is a version of an Italian mixture known as polenta.

½ cup yellow cornmeal
¼ teaspoon ground cumin
2 teaspoons butter *or* margarine
1 pound lean ground beef
1 cup chopped onion
1 cup chopped green *or* sweet red pepper
½ cup chopped carrot
1 clove garlic, minced
2 teaspoons chili powder
1 15-ounce can tomato sauce
1 12-ounce can whole kernel corn, drained
1 4-ounce can chopped green chili peppers, drained
½ cup sliced pitted ripe olives

● In a small saucepan combine cornmeal, cumin, 1¼ cups cold *water,* ¼ teaspoon *salt,* and ⅛ teaspoon *pepper.* Bring just to boiling; reduce the heat. Stir in butter or margarine. Cook over low heat for 10 minutes, stirring often. Remove from the heat. Spread mixture on waxed paper into an 8-inch square. Chill.

● In a large skillet cook beef, onion, green pepper, carrot, garlic, and chili powder till meat is brown and onion is tender; drain. Stir in tomato sauce, corn, green chili peppers, and olives.

● Spoon mixture into a 12x7½x2-inch baking dish. Cut cornmeal mixture into desired shapes, piecing together scraps, if necessary. Place on top of meat mixture. Seal, label, and freeze.

● **To serve,** bake frozen casserole, covered, in a 375° oven about 1½ hours or till heated through. Makes 6 servings.

Beef Steaks Wellington

If a few of the pastry cutouts fall off when you remove the bundles from the freezer, simply remoisten and put them back on before baking.

1   17¼-ounce package
      (2 sheets) frozen
      puff pastry
8   5-ounce beef tenderloin
      steaks, cut 1 inch thick
1   tablespoon cooking oil
1   4¾-ounce can liver pâté
¼   cup soft bread crumbs
1   tablespoon snipped parsley
½   teaspoon dried basil,
      crushed
¼   teaspoon garlic salt
      Dash pepper
1   cup sliced fresh mushrooms
¼   cup sliced green onion
2   tablespoons butter *or*
      margarine
2   teaspoons cornstarch
¼   cup dry white wine
¼   cup water
1   teaspoon instant beef
      bouillon granules

● Thaw pastry according to package directions. Meanwhile, in a large skillet brown steaks in hot oil over medium-high heat for 1 minute on each side. Drain on paper towels. Cool. Stir together pâté, crumbs, parsley, basil, garlic salt, and pepper. Spread 1 rounded tablespoon of pâté mixture on top of each steak.

● Roll each sheet of puff pastry into an 11-inch square; cut each into four 5½-inch squares. Place pastry squares on top of steaks; fold under meat. If necessary, trim pastry so only ½ inch remains folded under the meat. Reserve any pastry trimmings.

● Place steak bundles on a baking sheet. If desired, cut small shapes from pastry trimmings; moisten and place on top of bundles. Cover and freeze about 1 hour or till firm. Transfer to freezer bags or containers. Seal, label, and freeze.

● **To serve,** place frozen bundles, pastry side up, on a rack in a shallow baking pan. Bake, uncovered, in a preheated 450° oven about 25 minutes or till pastry is brown and meat is medium-rare. If necessary, cover loosely with foil during the last 5 minutes to prevent overbrowning.

● Meanwhile, prepare sauce. In a medium saucepan cook mushrooms and onion in butter or margarine till tender. Stir in cornstarch. Add wine, water, and bouillon granules. Cook and stir till thickened and bubbly, then cook and stir for 2 minutes more. Serve with meat. Makes 8 servings.

Assembling the Beef Steaks Wellington

Place the pastry squares on top of the steaks and fold the pastry under the meat. (If necessary, trim the pastry to leave just ½ inch under the meat on all sides.) For a decorative look, cut small shapes out of the pastry trimmings and place these cutouts on top of the bundles.

The bottom of the meat is not wrapped entirely in pastry because the juices that run out of the meat during reheating would make the pastry soggy.

Swiss Steak

In this case, "Swiss" is an old-fashioned term for tenderizing.

1½ pounds beef round steak, cut ½ inch thick
2 tablespoons cooking oil
1 16-ounce can tomatoes, cut up
1 small onion, sliced
1 stalk celery, sliced
1 medium carrot, thinly sliced
2 tablespoons cold water
1 tablespoon cornstarch
½ teaspoon Worcestershire sauce
3 cups hot cooked rice *or* noodles

● Cut meat into 6 serving-size pieces. Pound both sides of meat lightly to tenderize. In a large skillet brown *half* of the meat in *1 tablespoon* hot oil for 4 minutes, turning once. Remove from the skillet. Brown remaining meat in remaining oil. Drain off fat. Return all of the meat to the skillet. Stir in *undrained* tomatoes, onion, celery, and carrot. Bring to boiling; reduce the heat. Cover and simmer about 1 hour or till meat is tender.

● Stir together water, cornstarch, and Worcestershire sauce. Add to skillet; cook and stir till thickened and bubbly, then cook and stir for 2 minutes more. Remove from the heat; cool. Spoon into a 1½-quart freezer container. Seal, label, and freeze.

● **To serve,** transfer frozen mixture to a medium saucepan. Cover and cook over medium-low heat about 45 minutes or till heated through, stirring occasionally. Serve with cooked rice or noodles. Makes 6 servings.

Shrimp-Swiss Patty Shells

You can thaw the shrimp while the frozen mixture is reheating. Just place them in a colander under running water, then drain well and blot dry with paper towels.

1½ cups milk
3 tablespoons cornstarch
1 2½-ounce jar sliced mushrooms
¼ teaspoon paprika
⅛ teaspoon pepper
2 cups shredded process Swiss cheese (8 ounces)
1 10-ounce package frozen peas with pearl onions
½ cup dry white wine
1 16-ounce package frozen peeled and deveined shrimp, thawed and well drained
1 10-ounce package (6) frozen patty shells

● In a medium saucepan stir together milk and cornstarch. Add mushrooms, paprika, and pepper. Cook and stir till thickened and bubbly, then cook and stir for 2 minutes more.

● Add cheese to milk mixture. Cook and stir till cheese melts; remove from the heat. Stir in peas with onions and wine. Cool. Spoon into a 1½-quart freezer container. Seal, label, and freeze.

● **To serve,** transfer frozen mixture to a large saucepan. Cover and cook over medium-low heat about 30 minutes or till thawed, stirring frequently. Add shrimp; cook and stir for 8 to 10 minutes more or till shrimp is tender and mixture is heated through. Meanwhile, bake patty shells according to package directions. Spoon shrimp mixture into patty shells. Garnish with fresh kale, if desired. Serve immediately. Makes 6 servings.

Newburg-Style Lobster

It's every bit as elegant as it sounds!

1 pound lobster meat, chopped (about 1½ pounds lobster tails)
2 tablespoons butter or margarine
¼ cup dry sherry
¼ cup butter or margarine
2 tablespoons cornstarch
1 teaspoon finely shredded lemon peel
¼ teaspoon salt
Dash ground red pepper
2 cups light cream
6 slices of bread or 6 frozen patty shells
Snipped chives (optional)

● In a medium saucepan cook lobster in 2 tablespoons butter or margarine for 2 minutes, stirring frequently. Add sherry and cook for 1 minute more. Remove from the saucepan.

● In the same saucepan melt ¼ cup butter or margarine. Stir in cornstarch, lemon peel, salt, and red pepper. Add cream all at once. Cook and stir till thickened and bubbly, then cook and stir 2 minutes more. Stir in lobster mixture. Cool. Transfer to a 1½-quart freezer container. Seal, label, and freeze.

● **To serve,** transfer frozen mixture to a large saucepan. Cover and cook over medium-low heat about 40 minutes or till heated through, stirring occasionally. Meanwhile, toast bread and cut each slice in half diagonally or bake patty shells according to package directions. Spoon lobster mixture over toast points or into shells. Sprinkle with chives, if desired. Makes 6 servings.

Shrimp-Swiss Patty Shells

Spicy Tuna Casserole

1 cup elbow macaroni
½ cup sliced celery
¼ cup chopped onion
1½ teaspoons cooking oil
1 10-ounce can tomatoes and green chili peppers
1 7½-ounce can semi-condensed cream of mushroom soup
2 cups loose-pack frozen mixed vegetables
½ cup shredded cheddar cheese (2 ounces)
½ teaspoon dried basil, crushed
¼ teaspoon dried marjoram, crushed
¼ teaspoon dried thyme, crushed
⅛ teaspoon ground red pepper
1 6½-ounce can tuna, drained and broken into pieces
⅓ cup crushed rye crackers

● Cook macaroni in boiling unsalted water for 5 to 6 minutes or till almost tender; drain. Meanwhile, in a medium saucepan cook celery and onion in hot oil till tender. Stir in tomatoes and soup. Add vegetables, cheese, basil, marjoram, thyme, red pepper, and macaroni; stir till well combined. Gently stir in tuna. Spoon mixture into a 2-quart casserole. Seal, label, and freeze.

● **To serve,** bake frozen casserole, covered, in a 375° oven about 1¼ hours or till nearly heated through, stirring occasionally. Uncover and sprinkle with crushed crackers. Bake for 5 to 10 minutes more or till heated through. Makes 4 servings.

Salmon and Cheese Casserole

3 tablespoons butter *or* margarine
2 tablespoons cornstarch
¾ teaspoon dried basil, crushed
¼ teaspoon pepper
2 cups milk
1½ cups loose-pack frozen mixed broccoli, carrots, and cauliflower
2 cups cooked brown rice
1 4-ounce can sliced mushrooms, drained
½ cup shredded American cheese (2 ounces)
1 15-ounce can salmon

● In a large saucepan melt butter or margarine. Stir in cornstarch, basil, and pepper. Add milk all at once. Cook and stir till thickened and bubbly, then cook and stir for 2 minutes more. Stir in cheese. Cook and stir till cheese melts.

● Cut up any large frozen vegetables. Stir frozen vegetables, rice, and mushrooms into the thickened mixture. Drain and flake salmon, discarding skin and bones. Gently stir the salmon into the rice mixture. Spoon into a greased 2-quart casserole. Seal, label, and freeze.

● **To serve,** bake the frozen casserole, covered, in a 375° oven about 1½ hours or till the mixture is heated through, stirring occasionally. Makes 4 servings.

Microwave Reheating Chart

Use the timings listed at right as a guide for reheating frozen foods in a microwave oven. You can apply the timings to similar recipes in this chapter or to your own recipes.

Here's how the chart works. If you want to reheat a frozen meat and vegetable stir-fry dish, such as chicken chow mein, micro-cook 1 cup of the mixture about 7 minutes, 2 cups about 11 minutes, or 3 cups about 19 minutes. All frozen foods were reheated on 70% power (MEDIUM-HIGH), stirring occasionally.

Mixture	1 cup	2 cups	3 cups
Beef Stroganoff	5 min.	10 min.	15 min.
Chicken chow mein	7 min.	11 min.	19 min.
Lobster Newburg	5 min.	11 min.	16 min.
Macaroni and cheese	8 min.	13½ min.	18 min.
Roast beef with gravy	11 min.	16 min.	20 min.
Spaghetti and meat sauce	7 min.	12 min.	18 min.
Tuna-noodle casserole	5 min.	8 min.	12 min.

Savory Stuffed Peppers

To cut the baking time to 40 minutes, thaw the peppers overnight in the refrigerator.

3 large green peppers
¼ cup chopped carrot
¼ cup sliced green onion
2 teaspoons cooking oil
1 15-ounce can corned beef hash
1 8¾-ounce can whole kernel corn, drained
⅓ cup shredded cheddar cheese

● Cut peppers in half lengthwise. Remove seeds and membranes. In a skillet cook carrot and onion in hot oil till tender. Stir in hash and corn. Spoon hash mixture into peppers. Place in a shallow baking dish. Seal, label, and freeze.

● **To serve,** bake frozen peppers, covered, in a 375° oven about 1 hour or till heated through. Sprinkle with cheese before serving. Makes 3 servings.

Deep-Dish Spinach Pizza
(see recipe, page 36)

Sausage and
Mushroom Pizza

Sausage and Mushroom Pizzas

Try the Canadian bacon and sauerkraut version, too (only 299 calories per serving). It was a hit with our skeptical food editors.

1½ to 2 cups all-purpose flour
¾ cup whole wheat flour
¼ cup yellow cornmeal
1 package active dry yeast
½ teaspoon salt
1 cup warm water (115°
    to 120°)
2 tablespoons cooking oil
    Yellow cornmeal
2 8-ounce cans pizza sauce
½ cup grated Parmesan cheese
1 pound bulk Italian sausage,
    cooked and drained
1 4-ounce can sliced
    mushrooms, drained
3 cups shredded mozzarella
    cheese (12 ounces)

● In a small mixer bowl stir together ½ *cup* all-purpose flour, whole wheat flour, ¼ cup cornmeal, yeast, and salt. Add warm water and oil.

● Beat with an electric mixer on low speed for 30 seconds, scraping the sides of the bowl. Beat for 3 minutes on high speed. Using a spoon, stir in as much of the remaining all-purpose flour as you can.

● Turn dough out onto a lightly floured surface. Knead in enough remaining all-purpose flour to make a moderately stiff dough that is smooth and elastic (6 to 8 minutes total).

● Divide dough in half. Cover and let rest for 10 minutes. Sprinkle two 12-inch greased pizza pans with additional cornmeal. On a lightly floured surface roll each half of dough into a 13-inch circle; transfer to pans. Build up edges. Prick crust all over with a fork. Bake in a 425° oven for 10 minutes. Cool.

● Spread pizza sauce over pizza crusts; sprinkle with Parmesan cheese. Top with cooked sausage and mushrooms, then mozzarella cheese. Seal, label, and freeze.

● **To serve,** bake frozen pizzas, uncovered, in a 425° oven for 20 to 25 minutes or till crust is brown and topping is heated through. Makes 2 pizzas.

Canadian Bacon and Sauerkraut Pizzas: Prepare Sausage and Mushroom Pizzas as directed above, *except* omit sausage and mushrooms. After spreading pizza sauce on crusts and sprinkling with Parmesan cheese, top pizzas with 1 pound *Canadian-style bacon,* chopped; one 8-ounce can *sauerkraut,* rinsed, drained, and snipped; and 2 cups shredded *mozzarella cheese.* Continue as directed.

Lasagna for a Crowd

Have this ready when you know the hungry troops are coming.

1 pound bulk pork sausage
½ cup chopped onion
1 clove garlic, minced
1 16-ounce can tomatoes, cut up
1 8-ounce can tomato sauce
1 6-ounce can tomato paste
2 teaspoons dried basil, crushed
8 ounces lasagna noodles (8 noodles)
2 beaten eggs
2½ cups ricotta *or* drained cream-style cottage cheese
¾ cup grated Parmesan cheese
2 tablespoons snipped parsley
½ teaspoon pepper
12 ounces mozzarella cheese, thinly sliced

● In a large skillet cook meat, onion, and garlic till meat is brown and onion is tender. Drain off fat. Stir in tomatoes, tomato sauce, tomato paste, and basil. Bring to boiling; reduce the heat. Cover and simmer for 15 minutes, stirring often.

● Meanwhile, cook noodles according to package directions; drain. Rinse with cold water; drain. In a small mixing bowl stir together eggs, ricotta or cottage cheese, *½ cup* of the Parmesan cheese, parsley, and pepper.

● To assemble, arrange *one-fourth* of the noodles in the bottom of a greased 8x8x2-inch or a 12x7½x2-inch baking dish, trimming to fit. Spread with *one-fourth* of the ricotta mixture. Top with *one-fourth* of the mozzarella cheese and *one-fourth* of the meat sauce. Repeat layers once. Sprinkle with *half* of the remaining Parmesan cheese. Assemble remaining ingredients the same way in another greased 8x8x2-inch or 12x7½x2-inch baking dish. Sprinkle with the remaining Parmesan cheese. Seal, label, and freeze.

● **To serve,** thaw lasagna overnight in the refrigerator. Bake, covered, in a 375° oven about 1½ hours or till heated through. Let stand 5 minutes. Makes two 6-serving portions.

Curried Pork

1 pound boneless pork
1 tablespoon cooking oil
1 large apple, cored and chopped
¼ cup sliced green onion
2 teaspoons curry powder
1 10¾-ounce can condensed cream of mushroom soup
¾ cup milk
2 tablespoons snipped parsley
1 8-ounce carton dairy sour cream
2 cups hot cooked brown rice

● Partially freeze pork. Cut on the bias into thin bite-size strips. Preheat a large skillet or wok over high heat. Add oil. (Add more oil as necessary during cooking.) Stir-fry *half* of the pork in hot oil for 2 minutes. Remove from skillet. Stir-fry remaining pork for 2 minutes. Remove from skillet, reserving drippings.

● In the same skillet cook apple, onion, and curry powder in reserved drippings till onion is tender. Stir in soup, milk, parsley, and pork. Remove from heat; cool. Spoon mixture into a 1½-quart freezer container. Seal, label, and freeze.

● **To serve,** transfer frozen mixture to a medium saucepan. Cover and cook over medium heat about 50 minutes or till heated through, stirring occasionally. Stir in sour cream; heat through. *Do not boil.* Serve over rice. Makes 4 servings.

Vegetarian Quiche

Be careful not to break or crack the pastry shell while it's stored in the freezer.

1¼ cups all-purpose flour
¼ teaspoon salt
⅓ cup shortening *or* lard
3 to 4 tablespoons cold water
½ cup shredded Swiss cheese
½ cup shredded cheddar
  cheese
½ cup shredded carrot
⅓ cup sliced green onion
1 tablespoon all-purpose flour
4 slightly beaten eggs
1½ cups light cream *or* milk
¼ teaspoon salt
⅛ teaspoon pepper
⅛ teaspoon garlic powder

● In a bowl combine flour and ¼ teaspoon salt. Cut in shortening till pieces are the size of small peas. Sprinkle *1 tablespoon* water over part of mixture; toss with a fork. Push to side of the bowl. Repeat till all is moistened. Form into a ball. On a lightly floured surface roll dough from center to edge, forming a 12-inch circle. Fit into a 9-inch pie plate. Trim pastry to ½ inch beyond edge of pie plate; flute edge high. Do not prick pastry.

● Line pastry shell with a double thickness of heavy-duty foil. Bake in a 450° oven for 7 minutes. Remove foil; bake for 3 to 5 minutes more or till pastry starts to brown. Cool. Toss together cheeses, carrot, green onion, and flour. Sprinkle mixture over the bottom of the pastry shell. Seal, label, and freeze.

● **To serve,** combine eggs, cream or milk, ¼ teaspoon salt, pepper, and garlic powder. Pour into frozen shell. Bake in a 375° oven for 35 to 45 minutes or till a knife inserted near the center comes out clean. Let stand for 10 minutes. Makes 6 servings.

Preparing the quiche
After partially baking and cooling the pastry shell, sprinkle cheeses, carrot, and green onion in the bottom of the shell. Then seal, label, and freeze. When you're ready to bake the quiche, stir together the egg-cream mixture and pour it directly over the frozen cheese mixture in the pastry shell.

The egg-cream mixture is not frozen with the other ingredients to prevent the outside edges of the quiche from overcooking before the center is done.

Deep-Dish Spinach Pizza

A meatless meal that won't leave you hungry. (Pictured on page 32.)

1   16-ounce loaf frozen
      bread dough, thawed
2   10-ounce packages frozen
      chopped spinach
¼   cup chopped onion
1   tablespoon butter *or*
      margarine
1   beaten egg
1   15-ounce carton ricotta
      cheese
⅔   cup grated Parmesan cheese
1   8-ounce can pizza sauce
1½ cups shredded Swiss *or*
      mozzarella cheese
      (6 ounces)

● Let dough rise according to package directions; punch down. Cover; let rest 5 minutes. Line a 13x9x2-inch baking pan with heavy-duty foil; grease foil on bottom and 1 inch up sides. Roll dough into a 14x10-inch rectangle. Pat onto bottom and 1 inch up sides of pan. Prick bottom and sides of dough. Bake in a 425° oven about 10 minutes or till dough starts to brown; cool.

● Meanwhile, cook spinach according to package directions; drain well. In a small skillet cook onion in butter till tender. Combine egg, ricotta, Parmesan, spinach, and onion mixture. Spread over pizza crust. Pour pizza sauce over all. Freeze for 1½ to 2 hours or till firm. Lift pizza out of pan. Cover the top with clear plastic wrap. Seal in heavy-duty foil, label, and freeze.

● **To serve,** place frozen pizza on a baking sheet. Remove top foil and plastic wrap. Fold back bottom foil, leaving sides covered. Bake in a 375° oven for 60 to 65 minutes or till heated through. Top with cheese. Bake about 10 minutes more or till cheese melts. Let stand 5 minutes; remove foil. Makes 1 pizza.

Freezer Menus

Menu
Stuffed Chicken Rolls
(see recipe, page 23)
• • •
Wild Rice Pilaf
(see recipe, page 67)
• • •
Steamed asparagus
• • •
Lettuce with dressing
• • •
Chocolate Layered Trifle
(see recipe, page 84)

Most of the recipes in this book that call for oven reheating require a 375° oven. And for good reason. If you're reheating a frozen main dish and want to reheat a frozen side dish, too, you can use the same oven at the same temperature and serve them at the same time.

Here's a sample menu to show you how easy this is.

The day before your meal, thaw the Chocolate Layered Trifle for 24 hours in the refrigerator. Because the Stuffed Chicken Rolls take about 1½ hours to reheat, put six of them in the oven first. The Wild Rice Pilaf needs about 1 hour in the oven so put it in 30 minutes after the Stuffed Chicken Rolls. During the last 15 minutes of baking, steam the asparagus and tear or cut the lettuce into wedges. And there you have it! All of the food will be ready to eat at the same time. Top off your meal with the cool and creamy Chocolate Layered Trifle.

Ahh! There's nothing better than homemade soup or stew, especially when it is waiting in your freezer. Choose from a robust main-dish stew, a steamy side-dish soup, a hearty meat and vegetable soup, a creamy chowder, or a reduced-calorie soup. They're all here in this chapter. With any of these on hand, you'll have a quick answer to the "what's for dinner?" question.

Soup and Stew Tips

Soup Cubes

A convenient way to freeze cream and broth soups is by using plastic ice cube trays. Cool the soup and pour it into individual compartments of an ice cube tray. Simply freeze till the soup is completely firm, pop out the cubes of frozen soup, then store them in a freezer bag. This way you can reheat a few cubes of soup for a single serving, or more for the entire family.

Fat-Trimming Tips

With a few changes in the method and ingredients, you can cut down on the fat (and calories) in many of these recipes.

One of the best ways to slash fat from a soup or stew is to chill it before freezing. Any fat will harden and rise to the surface as the soup cools. Then simply skim it off the top.

Another easy way to reduce fat is by using low-fat ingredients. Buy lean meats and trim them of any separable fat, substitute skim or evaporated skimmed milk for whole milk, top the soup or stew with plain low-fat yogurt instead of sour cream, and cook or garnish with low-fat versions of hard cheeses.

"Souper" Toppers

Not only can you keep soup or stew on hand in the freezer, but you can store some terrific toppers, too. Freeze a handful of shredded cheese to toss on a thick bean soup. Sprinkle snipped parsley or chives from the freezer over a bowl of creamy tomato soup. Garnish chowders and stews with toasted bread cubes or seasoned croutons, which also freeze well. You can even freeze unpopped popcorn. Then, while your soup or stew is reheating, pop up a batch of popcorn to float on individual servings. Store the toppers in moisture- and vaporproof freezer containers or bags.

How Long Will It Keep?

Soups and stews are always welcome on cold, blustery days, but they make delicious fair-weather meals, too. So if you're wondering whether the soup or stew you put in the freezer last fall is still good, keep in mind that it can be frozen for up to six months.

Zesty Seafood Gumbo

230 CALORIES SERVING

Gumbo is a Creole soup made with meat, poultry, or seafood and thickened with okra or gumbo filé. This one's stocked with shrimp, oysters, and okra.

2 medium onions, chopped
1 medium green pepper, chopped
2 tablespoons cooking oil
1 tablespoon all-purpose flour
2 16-ounce cans stewed tomatoes
1 10-ounce package frozen cut okra
1 6-ounce can tomato paste
½ cup water
1 teaspoon celery salt
½ teaspoon sugar
½ teaspoon garlic powder
½ teaspoon bottled hot pepper sauce
1 pound fresh *or* frozen shelled shrimp
1 8-ounce can whole oysters, drained

● In a large saucepan cook onion and green pepper in hot oil till tender. Stir in flour. Cook, stirring constantly, about 3 minutes or till flour is golden brown.

● Stir in tomatoes, okra, tomato paste, water, celery salt, sugar, garlic powder, hot pepper sauce, and ¼ teaspoon *pepper*. Bring to boiling; reduce heat. Cover and simmer for 15 minutes. Remove from heat. Add shrimp and oysters; cool. Spoon mixture into a 2- to 2½-quart freezer container. Seal, label, and freeze.

● **To serve,** transfer frozen mixture to a large saucepan. Cover and cook over medium-low heat about 1¼ hours or till heated through, stirring occasionally. Makes 6 servings.

Salmon Chowder

5 slices bacon, cut up
½ cup chopped onion
½ cup sliced celery
¼ cup chopped green pepper
1 clove garlic, minced
1 tablespoon instant chicken bouillon granules
1 15½-ounce can salmon, drained, flaked, and cartilage removed
1 12-ounce can (1½ cups) evaporated milk
1 10-ounce package frozen mixed vegetables
1 8½-ounce can cream-style corn
2 tablespoons snipped parsley
2 teaspoons dried dillweed
¼ teaspoon celery seed

● In a large skillet cook bacon till crisp. Drain on paper towels, reserving 1 tablespoon drippings in skillet. Cook onion, celery, green pepper, and garlic in reserved drippings till tender.

● In a large saucepan bring 2½ cups *water* and bouillon granules to boiling. Stir in bacon, onion mixture, salmon, milk, frozen vegetables, corn, parsley, dillweed, celery seed, and ⅛ teaspoon *pepper*. Remove from the heat; cool. Pour mixture into two 1-quart freezer containers. Seal, label, and freeze.

● **To serve,** transfer 1 portion of the frozen mixture to a large saucepan. Cover and cook over medium-low heat about 45 minutes or till heated through, stirring occasionally. Makes two 3-serving portions.

Herbed Fresh Tomato Soup

Pastry Twists
(see recipe, page 91)

Herbed Fresh Tomato Soup

If you can afford the calories, nibble on Pastry Twists while savoring this side-dish soup (70 calories per twist).

2 medium onions, thinly
   sliced
2 tablespoons olive oil *or*
   cooking oil
2½ cups water
6 medium tomatoes, peeled
   and quartered (about 2
   pounds)
1 6-ounce can tomato paste
2 tablespoons snipped fresh
   basil *or* 2 teaspoons dried
   basil, crushed
1 tablespoon snipped fresh
   thyme *or* 1 teaspoon dried
   thyme, crushed
1 tablespoon instant chicken
   bouillon granules
½ teaspoon sugar
½ teaspoon salt
¼ teaspoon pepper
   Few dashes bottled hot
   pepper sauce
   Snipped parsley

● In a large saucepan cook onion in hot oil till tender. Stir in water, tomatoes, tomato paste, basil, thyme, bouillon granules, sugar, salt, pepper, and hot pepper sauce. Bring to boiling; reduce the heat. Cover and simmer for 40 minutes.

● Place about one-third of the tomato mixture in a blender container or food processor bowl; cover and blend till smooth. (Or press mixture through a food mill.) Repeat with remaining mixture; cool. Pour mixture into two 3-cup freezer containers. Seal, label, and freeze.

● **To serve,** transfer 1 portion of the frozen mixture to a medium saucepan. Cover and cook over medium heat for 20 to 25 minutes or till heated through, stirring occasionally. Sprinkle with parsley before serving. Makes two 4-serving portions.

Minestrone

This traditional Italian soup is bursting with fresh vegetables, pasta, and beans.

  2 stalks celery, chopped
  1 large onion, chopped
  1 clove garlic, minced
  2 tablespoons olive oil *or*
       cooking oil
  3 cups water
  4 medium tomatoes, peeled
       and chopped, *or* one
       16-ounce can tomatoes,
       cut up
  2 tablespoons snipped parsley
  1 tablespoon instant beef
       bouillon granules
  1 bay leaf
1½ teaspoons dried basil,
       crushed
  ½ teaspoon dried oregano,
       crushed
  ⅛ teaspoon pepper
  1 cup sliced carrots
  1 15-ounce can red kidney
       beans
  1 9-ounce package frozen
       Italian green beans *or*
       cut green beans
  2 ounces spaghetti, broken
       into 1-inch pieces (½ cup)
     Grated Parmesan cheese

● In a Dutch oven cook celery, onion, and garlic in hot oil till tender. Add water, fresh or *undrained* tomatoes, parsley, bouillon granules, bay leaf, basil, oregano, and pepper.

● Bring to boiling; reduce the heat. Cover and simmer for 30 minutes. Add carrots. Cover and simmer for 5 minutes more. Remove from the heat. Remove bay leaf. Stir in kidney beans, green beans, and spaghetti. Cool. Pour mixture into two 1-quart freezer containers. Seal, label, and freeze.

● **To serve,** transfer 1 portion of frozen mixture to a medium saucepan. Cover and cook over medium heat for 40 to 45 minutes or till heated through, stirring occasionally. Sprinkle each serving with cheese. Makes two 4-serving portions.

French Onion Soup

You can toast the bread slices in your broiler for 1½ minutes per side.

3 large onions, thinly sliced
1 clove garlic, minced
¼ cup butter *or* margarine
3 10½-ounce cans condensed beef broth
2 cups water
6 1-inch slices French bread
6 1-ounce slices Swiss *or* Gruyère cheese
Grated Parmesan cheese

● In a large saucepan cook onion and garlic in butter or margarine, covered, over low heat about 20 minutes or till very tender. Stir occasionally; remove from heat. Stir in beef broth and water. Pour into a 2-quart freezer container. Seal, label, and freeze.

● **To serve,** transfer frozen mixture to a large saucepan. Cover and cook over medium heat about 25 minutes or till heated through, stirring occasionally.

● Meanwhile, toast bread slices; arrange on a baking sheet. Top bread with Swiss or Gruyère cheese. Sprinkle lightly with Parmesan cheese. Broil 3 to 4 inches from the heat for 2 to 3 minutes or till cheese is light brown and bubbly. Ladle hot soup into serving bowls. Top with bread slices. Makes 6 servings.

Broiling the bread and cheese

While the frozen soup is reheating, toast the slices of French bread. Just before serving, top each bread slice with a slice of cheese. Sprinkle lightly with the Parmesan cheese.

Broil the bread slices 3 to 4 inches from the heat for 2 to 3 minutes or till the cheese is light brown and bubbly. With a spatula, transfer one slice of bread to each individual bowl of soup.

Broccoli-Cheddar Chowder

So smooth, so rich, and so easy with canned cheddar cheese soup.

1½ cups milk
1 11-ounce can condensed cheddar cheese soup
1 cup frozen loose-pack chopped broccoli
½ cup frozen loose-pack hash brown potatoes
½ cup frozen whole kernel corn
2 tablespoons chopped pimiento

● In a medium saucepan stir together milk and soup. Cook and stir over medium heat till bubbly. Remove from the heat. Stir in broccoli, hash browns, corn, and pimiento; cool. Pour mixture into a 1-quart freezer container. Seal, label, and freeze.

● **To serve,** transfer frozen mixture to a large saucepan. Cover and cook over medium-low heat for 40 to 45 minutes or till heated through, stirring occasionally. Makes 6 servings.

Five-Bean Soup

Count 'em! Refried, red kidney, garbanzo, navy, and lima beans.

2 medium onions, chopped
2 cloves garlic, minced
1 tablespoon cooking oil
3½ cups chicken broth
1 16-ounce can refried beans
1 15½-ounce can red kidney beans, drained
1 15-ounce can garbanzo beans, drained
1 15-ounce can navy beans
1 12-ounce can beer
1 8½-ounce can lima beans
1 4-ounce can diced green chili peppers, drained
1 tablespoon paprika
1 tablespoon chili powder
1 tablespoon prepared mustard
½ teaspoon dried basil, crushed
½ teaspoon dried oregano, crushed
Croutons (optional)
Shredded Monterey Jack *or* cheddar cheese (optional)

● In a Dutch oven cook onion and garlic in hot oil till tender. Stir in chicken broth, refried beans, kidney beans, garbanzo beans, navy beans, beer, lima beans, chili peppers, paprika, chili powder, mustard, basil, and oregano.

● Bring to boiling; reduce the heat. Cover and simmer for 1 hour. Remove from the heat; cool. Pour mixture into two 1½-quart freezer containers. Seal, label, and freeze.

● **To serve,** transfer 1 portion of the frozen mixture to a large saucepan. Cover and cook over medium-low heat about 50 minutes or till heated through, stirring occasionally. Top each serving of soup with croutons and shredded cheese, if desired. Makes two 4-serving portions.

Broccoli-Cheddar Chowder

Oven Beef Stew

Serve with fresh hot biscuits to soak up every drop.

¼ cup all-purpose flour
1½ pounds beef stew meat, cut into 1-inch cubes
4 medium carrots, cut into 1-inch pieces
4 small onions, quartered
2 cups water
1 6-ounce can tomato paste
1 tablespoon vinegar
1 teaspoon sugar
2 cloves garlic, minced
½ teaspoon dried thyme, crushed
1 9-ounce package frozen cut green beans

● In a paper or plastic bag combine flour, 1 teaspoon *salt,* and ¼ teaspoon *pepper.* Add beef cubes, a few at a time. Shake bag to coat meat, using all of the flour mixture.

● In a 3-quart casserole combine beef, carrots, and onions. Stir together water, tomato paste, vinegar, sugar, garlic, and thyme; pour over meat mixture in the casserole. Cover and bake in a 350° oven for 1½ hours. Stir beans into meat mixture; cool. Seal, label, and freeze.

● **To serve,** bake frozen casserole, covered, in a 375° oven for 1¼ to 1½ hours or till heated through, stirring occasionally. Makes 8 servings.

Microwave
Reheating Chart

Use the timings listed at right as a guide for reheating frozen foods in a microwave oven. You can apply the timings to similar recipes in this chapter or to your own.

Here's how the chart works. If you want to reheat a frozen meaty stew, such as beef stew, micro-cook 1 cup of the mixture about 5½ minutes, 2 cups about 9½ minutes, or 3 cups about 14½ minutes. All frozen foods were reheated on 70% power (MEDIUM-HIGH), stirring occasionally.

Mixture	1 cup	2 cups	3 cups
Beef stew	5½ min.	9½ min.	14½ min.
Chicken broth	6½ min.	11½ min.	17 min.
Chicken soup	7 min.	12 min.	20 min.
Chili	6 min.	10½ min.	16 min.
Clam chowder	5 min.	11 min.	14½ min.
Tomato soup	5 min.	13 min.	15 min.

Mexican Beer Chowder

1 pound ground beef
1 medium onion, chopped
1 clove garlic, minced
1 16-ounce can tomatoes
1 16-ounce can refried beans
1 12-ounce can beer
1 12-ounce can whole kernel corn, drained
1 4-ounce can diced green chili peppers, drained
2 tablespoons chili powder
2 tablespoons Worcestershire sauce
½ teaspoon ground cumin
2 cups tortilla chips
1 8-ounce carton dairy sour cream
1 cup shredded cheddar cheese (4 ounces)

● In a Dutch oven cook beef, onion, and garlic till meat is brown and onion is tender; drain. Cut up tomatoes. Stir *undrained* tomatoes, refried beans, beer, corn, chili peppers, chili powder, Worcestershire sauce, cumin, and 1 cup *water* into meat mixture. Bring to boiling; reduce the heat. Cover and simmer for 20 minutes; cool. Pour into a 2-quart freezer container. Seal, label, and freeze.

● **To serve,** transfer frozen mixture to a large saucepan. Cover and cook over medium-low heat about 1 hour or till heated through, stirring occasionally. Arrange chips in soup bowls. Spoon hot meat mixture over chips. Sprinkle with cheese and dollop with sour cream. Makes 6 servings.

Serving the Mexican Beer Chowder

To serve the meaty chowder, arrange tortilla chips in six individual soup bowls. Spoon the hot chowder over tortilla chips. Sprinkle each serving with cheddar cheese and dollop with sour cream. Be sure to serve the soup right away—before the tortilla chips get soggy.

Brunswick Stew

352 CALORIES SERVING

This popular plantation stew was originally made with rabbit.

1   3- to 3½-pound broiler-fryer
    chicken, cut up and
    skinned
6   cups water
1   bay leaf
1   teaspoon salt
1   teaspoon dried rosemary,
    crushed
2   medium potatoes, peeled
    and cubed
1   large onion, chopped
1   17-ounce can cream-style
    corn
1   16-ounce can tomatoes, cut
    up
1   10-ounce package frozen
    cut okra
1   10-ounce package frozen
    lima beans
1   6-ounce can tomato paste
½   teaspoon pepper

● In a 6-quart Dutch oven combine chicken, water, bay leaf, salt, and rosemary. Bring to boiling; reduce the heat. Cover and simmer about 1 hour or till chicken is tender. Remove chicken from Dutch oven. Remove bay leaf.

● When chicken is cool enough to handle, remove meat from bones. Cut meat into bite-size pieces; return to Dutch oven. Stir in potatoes, onion, corn, tomatoes, okra, beans, tomato paste, and pepper. Pour mixture into two 2-quart freezer containers. Seal, label, and freeze.

● **To serve,** transfer 1 portion of the frozen mixture to a large saucepan. Cover and cook over medium-low heat about 1 hour or till heated through, stirring occasionally. Simmer the mixture about 5 minutes more or till potatoes are tender. Makes two 4-serving portions.

Chicken-Pea Pod Soup

126 CALORIES SERVING

*Add the pea pods the last few minutes of reheating
so they don't overcook.*

2   medium carrots, bias-sliced
    ¼ inch thick
1   medium onion, chopped
2   cloves garlic, minced
1   tablespoon cooking oil
3   cups chicken broth
2   whole large chicken breasts,
    skinned and halved
    lengthwise
½   teaspoon dried basil,
    crushed
¼   teaspoon dried marjoram,
    crushed
⅛   teaspoon pepper
1   6-ounce package frozen pea
    pods

● In a Dutch oven cook carrot, onion, and garlic in hot oil till onion is tender. Stir in chicken broth, chicken, basil, marjoram, and pepper. Bring to boiling; reduce the heat. Cover and simmer for 15 to 20 minutes or till chicken is tender. Remove from heat.

● Remove chicken from Dutch oven. When chicken is cool enough to handle, remove meat from bones. Cut meat into bite-size pieces; return to Dutch oven. Cool mixture; pour into a 1½-quart freezer container. Seal, label, and freeze.

● **To serve,** transfer frozen mixture to a Dutch oven. Cover and cook over medium-low heat for 50 to 60 minutes or till heated through, stirring occasionally. Stir in pea pods; cover and cook about 2 minutes more or till crisp-tender. Makes 6 servings.

Brunswick Stew

Oriental Pork Stew

Old-fashioned stew with a fresh, ethnic flavor.

2	pounds boneless pork, cut into ¾-inch cubes
2	tablespoons cooking oil
1¼	cups beef broth
1	large onion, chopped
⅓	cup catsup
3	tablespoons vinegar
2	teaspoons Worcestershire sauce
¾	cup beef broth
¼	cup all-purpose flour
4	medium carrots, cut into julienne strips
1	8-ounce can sliced water chestnuts, drained
1	6-ounce package frozen pea pods

● In a Dutch oven brown meat, half at a time, in hot oil. Return all meat to Dutch oven. Stir in 1¼ cups broth, onion, catsup, vinegar, Worcestershire sauce, and ¼ teaspoon *pepper*. Bring to boiling; reduce the heat. Cover and simmer about 40 minutes or just till meat is tender, stirring occasionally.

● Stir together ¾ cup beef broth and flour; add to Dutch oven. Cook and stir till thickened and bubbly, then cook and stir for 1 minute more. Remove from the heat. Stir in carrots and water chestnuts; cool. Pour mixture into two 1-quart freezer containers. Seal, label, and freeze.

● **To serve,** transfer 1 of the frozen portions to a medium saucepan. Cover and cook over low heat for 25 to 30 minutes or till heated through, stirring occasionally. Add *half* of the pea pods. Cover and cook about 2 minutes more or till crisp-tender. Serve with cooked rice, if desired. Makes two 4-serving portions.

Spicy Ham and Bean Soup

Some like it hot! If that's you, then use ½ teaspoon crushed red pepper.

1	small onion, chopped
1	small green pepper, chopped
¼	cup sliced carrot
¼	cup sliced celery
1	clove garlic, minced
1	tablespoon cooking oil
¼	cup brown rice
1	bay leaf
2	teaspoons instant chicken bouillon granules
½	teaspoon dried oregano, crushed
½	teaspoon dried thyme, crushed
¼ to ½	teaspoon crushed red pepper
1	16-ounce can tomatoes, cut up
1	15-ounce can red kidney beans, drained
1	cup diced fully cooked lean ham

● In a large saucepan cook onion, green pepper, carrot, celery, and garlic in hot oil till tender. Stir in rice, bay leaf, bouillon granules, oregano, thyme, red pepper, and 2 cups *water*.

● Bring to boiling; reduce the heat. Cover and simmer for 30 minutes. Remove from the heat. Remove bay leaf. Stir in *un-drained* tomatoes, beans, and ham; cool. Pour into a 1½-quart freezer container. Seal, label, and freeze.

● **To serve,** transfer frozen mixture to a large saucepan. Cover and cook over medium-low heat about 50 minutes or till heated through, stirring occasionally. Makes 4 servings.

SANDWICHES

The word "sandwich" can mean different things to different people. That's the beauty of it! In this chapter you'll find a variety of sandwiches and fillings to tempt your taste buds. You might try the snappy spin-off of a simple peanut butter sandwich or the tangy shredded pork mixture on a bun. Whatever you prefer, you'll find plenty of recipes that fit your fancy.

Sandwich Tips

To Freeze or Not to Freeze

Sandwiches can be almost anything you can fit between bread. But when you want to fix-and-freeze your sandwich, remember that some ingredients don't freeze well. Here are some common sandwich foods that shouldn't be frozen if they're the major part of a sandwich.

- Mayonnaise
- Dairy sour cream
- Yogurt
- Hard-cooked egg whites
- Fresh vegetables such as lettuce, celery, tomatoes, watercress, and cucumbers.

You can still enjoy these foods on frozen-and-thawed sandwiches by adding them just before eating.

Brown Bag Safety Tips

There's more to toting your lunch than tossing food in a bag. For the best flavor and utmost safety, keep hot foods hot and cold foods cold. Follow our simple suggestions to help keep your lunch safe and fresh-tasting for hours.

- When you prepare lunch, make sure anything that touches the food is clean.
- Seal foods in clean airtight containers or clear plastic storage bags.
- Thaw frozen sandwiches or fillings overnight in the refrigerator. Then, in the morning, pack them in insulated lunch boxes with frozen ice packs. Or pack a frozen sandwich in your bag in the morning; by lunchtime, it should be ready to eat.
- You can also pack hot or cold foods in insulated vacuum bottles. The bottles work best if you preheat or prechill them. To preheat (or prechill), fill the insulated vacuum bottle with very hot (or very cold) tap water. Cover with the lid and let stand 5 minutes. Empty the bottle and fill it with the hot (or cold) food.
- Make sure foods that require no heating or chilling are well wrapped.
- Use new lunch bags or clean lunch boxes.
- Keep your lunch in a cool dry place all morning.
- If you can, store your lunch in a refrigerator.

How Long Will It Keep?

It's nice to have sandwiches and sandwich fillings made ahead and frozen. But don't waste that extra effort by freezing them too long. As a general guide, you can freeze foods in this chapter for up to one month.

Peanut Butter and Cream Cheese Sandwiches

Spreading a little butter or margarine on the bread prevents it from getting soggy.

1 3-ounce package cream
    cheese, softened
1 tablespoon milk
2 teaspoons Worcestershire
    sauce
1 cup sliced celery
¼ cup shredded carrot
1 tablespoon sesame seed,
    toasted
    Pinch dried oregano,
    crushed
8 slices whole wheat bread
    Butter *or* margarine
    Chunk-style peanut butter

● In a small mixing bowl stir together cream cheese, milk, and Worcestershire sauce till smooth. Stir in celery, carrot, sesame seed, and oregano.

● Spread *1* side of *each* slice of bread lightly with butter or margarine. Spread cream cheese mixture on the buttered side of *4* slices of bread. Spread peanut butter on the buttered side of remaining slices of bread. Place slices of cream cheese mixture and peanut butter together to form 4 sandwiches. Wrap in moisture- and vaporproof wrap. Seal, label, and freeze.

● **To serve,** thaw sandwiches overnight in the refrigerator or let sandwiches stand at room temperature about 2½ hours or till thawed. Makes 4 servings.

Chicken and Rice Pitas

(181 CALORIES SERVING)

An excellent luncheon choice that doesn't harm the waistline. (Pictured on page 55.)

¾ cup water
⅓ cup brown rice
½ teaspoon instant chicken
    bouillon granules
1½ cups chopped cooked
    chicken *or* turkey
1 cup frozen chopped
    broccoli, cooked and
    drained
½ cup shredded cheddar
    cheese (2 ounces)
¼ cup shredded carrot
¼ cup sliced pitted ripe olives
1 8-ounce carton plain
    low-fat yogurt
2 tablespoons Dijon-style
    mustard
1 tablespoon honey
¼ teaspoon pepper
2 large pita bread rounds,
    halved crosswise
½ of a medium tomato, cut
    into 2 slices

● In a small saucepan stir together water, rice, and bouillon granules. Bring to boiling; reduce heat. Cover and simmer about 45 minutes or till rice is tender.

● Meanwhile, combine chicken, broccoli, cheese, carrot, and olives. Add rice mixture. Stir together yogurt, mustard, honey, and pepper. Pour over rice mixture, tossing to coat. Spoon mixture into two 2-cup freezer containers. Seal, label, and freeze.

● **To serve,** thaw 1 container of chicken mixture overnight in the refrigerator. Spoon about ½ cup of mixture into each pita half. Cut tomato slices in half; place in each pita half. Makes two 4-serving portions.

Turkey-Curry Croissants

Freeze the fruity curry filling separately. After it's thawed, assemble the sandwiches.

1   8¾-ounce can peach slices
1   cup finely chopped cooked
       turkey *or* chicken
¼   cup finely chopped celery
2   tablespoons snipped raisins
1   3-ounce package cream
       cheese, softened
½   teaspoon curry powder
4   croissants, split,
       or 8 slices bread
¼   cup chopped peanuts
       Lettuce leaves

● Drain and chop peaches, reserving *2 tablespoons* liquid. In a medium mixing bowl combine peaches, turkey or chicken, celery, and raisins.

● In a small mixing bowl stir together cream cheese, curry powder, and reserved peach liquid till smooth. Pour over turkey mixture, tossing to coat. Spoon the mixture into a 2-cup freezer container. Seal, label, and freeze.

● **To serve,** thaw turkey mixture overnight in the refrigerator. Spread mixture on 4 croissant bottoms or bread slices. Sprinkle with peanuts, then add lettuce. Cap with croissant tops or remaining bread slices. Makes 4 servings.

Shrimp-Stuffed Buns

To serve these cold, simply thaw the buns overnight in the refrigerator.

1   16-ounce package hot roll
       mix
2   3-ounce packages cream
       cheese with chives,
       softened
½   cup shredded Monterey
       Jack *or* Swiss cheese
       (2 ounces)
⅓   cup shredded carrot
2   tablespoons snipped parsley
½   teaspoon dried dillweed
⅛   teaspoon pepper
3   4½-ounce cans shrimp,
       rinsed, drained, and
       chopped
       Sesame seed

● Prepare hot roll mix according to package directions just through the kneading step. Cover and let rest for 10 minutes. Meanwhile, for filling, in a medium mixing bowl stir together cheeses, carrot, parsley, dillweed, and pepper. Fold in shrimp.

● Divide dough into 16 portions; shape each into a ball. Roll each ball into a 4½-inch circle. Place about *2 tablespoons* filling on *each* circle of dough. Bring up sides of dough around filling; pinch edges of dough to seal.

● Place buns, seam side down, on greased baking sheets. Cover and let rise in a warm place for 15 minutes. Brush tops lightly with water; sprinkle with sesame seed. Bake in a 375° oven for 15 to 18 minutes or till brown. Cool on wire racks. Return buns to baking sheets. Freeze, uncovered, about 1 hour or till firm. Transfer buns to freezer bags. Seal, label, and freeze.

● **To serve,** remove buns from freezer bags; wrap in foil. Place frozen buns in a 350° oven for 20 to 25 minutes or till heated through. Makes 16 servings.

Turkey-Curry Croissants

Shrimp-Stuffed Buns

Chicken and Rice Pitas
(see recipe, page 53)

Crab Stuffed Rye Rounds (handwritten)

Crab-Stuffed Rye Rounds

Whirl extra bread in a blender and use the crumbs in recipes calling for soft bread crumbs.

4 **Rye Bread Rounds**
½ **of a 10-ounce package frozen cut asparagus**
1 **8-ounce package cream cheese, softened**
1 **6-ounce can crabmeat, drained, flaked, and cartilage removed**
2 **tablespoons finely chopped green onion**
2 **tablespoons milk**
4 **ounces cheddar cheese, sliced**

● Prepare Rye Bread Rounds. Cook asparagus according to package directions; drain and cool. In a small mixing bowl stir together *half* of the cream cheese, crabmeat, onion, and *1 tablespoon* of the milk till well combined. In another bowl stir together remaining cream cheese, remaining milk, and asparagus.

● Slice off the top of each bread round; save the tops. Hollow out the bread rounds, leaving ¼-inch shells. (Store excess bread in the freezer for another use.)

● To assemble, line the bottoms of the hollowed-out bread with *half* of the cheese slices, cutting to fit. Spread the asparagus mixture over cheese. Top with remaining cheese slices, cutting to fit. Spread the crab mixture over cheese. Cap with the top slices of bread. Seal in heavy-duty foil, label, and freeze.

● **To serve,** place the frozen bread rounds in the refrigerator for 14 to 18 hours or till thawed. Cut each stuffed round in half. Makes 8 servings.

Rye Bread Rounds: Using 2 cups *all-purpose flour* total, in a large mixer bowl stir together *1¼ cups* all-purpose flour and 1 package active *dry yeast.* In a small saucepan heat 1 cup *water,* ¼ cup packed *brown sugar,* 1 tablespoon *cooking oil,* and ½ teaspoon *salt* just till warm (115° to 120°); stir constantly. Add to flour mixture. Beat with an electric mixer on low speed for 30 seconds, scraping bowl. Beat for 3 minutes on high speed. Using a spoon, stir in 1¼ cups *rye flour* and as much of the remaining all-purpose flour as you can.

● Turn dough out onto a lightly floured surface. Knead in enough of the remaining all-purpose flour to make a moderately stiff dough that is smooth and elastic (6 to 8 minutes total). Shape into a ball. Place in a greased bowl; turn once. Cover; let rise in a warm place till double (1 to 1¼ hours).

● Punch down dough; divide into fourths. Cover and let rest for 10 minutes. Shape into four 4-inch round loaves. Place on greased baking sheets. Cover and let rise in a warm place till nearly double (20 to 30 minutes).

● With a sharp knife make a small X in the top of each loaf. Combine 1 beaten *egg white* and 1 tablespoon *water;* brush over loaves. Bake in a 350° oven for 20 to 25 minutes or till brown. Cool on wire racks.

1 Hollowing out the bread

With a sharp knife, slice off the top one-third of each bread round. Set the tops aside. Using a spoon, loosen bread about ¼ inch from the edge. Pull out the bread in each round, leaving a ¼-inch shell. Now the bread rounds are ready to be layered with cheese and fillings.

2 Serving the bread rounds

Thaw frozen bread rounds, wrapped in foil, in the refrigerator. This should take 14 to 18 hours. Then cut each round in half to make two servings.

Be sure to leave the foil on the bread rounds during thawing. This keeps them from drying out.

Barbecue-Style Pork Sandwiches

Our Test Kitchen home economists prefer to use a boneless pork shoulder roast because it's very tender after cooking and costs less than other pork cuts.

1 pound boneless pork, cut into 1-inch pieces
1½ cups water
2 8-ounce cans tomato sauce
1 cup chopped onion
¼ cup vinegar
2 tablespoons brown sugar
2 tablespoons Worcestershire sauce
2 cloves garlic, minced
1 tablespoon dry mustard
2 teaspoons chili powder
2 teaspoons dried basil, crushed
1 teaspoon paprika
½ teaspoon celery seed
  Several dashes bottled hot pepper sauce
6 hamburger buns

● In a large saucepan bring meat and water to boiling; reduce heat. Cover and simmer about 1¼ hours or till meat is very tender. Drain. Using 2 forks, finely shred the meat (you should have about 2 cups shredded meat).

● Meanwhile, in a medium saucepan combine tomato sauce, onion, vinegar, sugar, Worcestershire sauce, garlic, mustard, chili powder, basil, paprika, celery seed, and hot pepper sauce. Bring to boiling; reduce heat. Cover and simmer for 15 minutes. Stir in meat. Cover and simmer 15 minutes more; cool. Spoon into a 1-quart freezer container. Seal, label, and freeze.

● **To serve,** transfer frozen meat mixture to a medium saucepan; add ¼ cup *water*. Cover and cook over medium-low heat about 60 minutes or till heated through, stirring occasionally. Meanwhile, split and toast buns. Spoon mixture into buns. Makes 6 servings.

Beefy Bean Burrito Sandwiches

Wrap these Mexican-style sandwiches in foil so you can pop them right in the oven to reheat.

½ pound ground beef
¼ cup chopped onion
1 clove garlic, minced
½ of a 16-ounce can refried beans
2 tablespoons chopped canned green chili peppers
  Few dashes bottled hot pepper sauce
4 10-inch flour tortillas
1 cup shredded cheddar cheese (4 ounces)
  Taco sauce
  Shredded cheddar cheese (optional)
  Shredded lettuce (optional)

● In a medium skillet cook beef, onion, and garlic till meat is brown and onion is tender; drain off fat. Stir in beans, chili peppers, and hot pepper sauce till well combined. Set aside.

● Wrap tortillas in foil; heat in a 350° oven for 10 minutes. Unwrap tortillas and spoon about ½ *cup* meat mixture down center of *each* tortilla. Sprinkle with 1 cup cheese; roll up, leaving ends open. Seal in heavy-duty foil, label, and freeze.

● **To serve,** bake frozen sandwiches, wrapped in foil, in a 375° oven for 35 to 40 minutes or till heated through. Serve with taco sauce. Top with additional shredded cheddar cheese and lettuce, if desired. Makes 4 servings.

START WITH A BASE

Starting with a mixture that can be made into several different recipes is a unique make-ahead idea. All of the recipes in this chapter start with a concentrated base that is divided into portions and frozen. You simply thaw a portion at a time and use it in one of the easy recipes on the following pages. And, since the bases are concentrated, they take minimal freezer space.

Start with a base . . .

This thick and zesty tomato base starts you on your way toward making three mouth-watering recipes. Choose among a savory clam chowder, a saucy spaghetti and meatballs dish, and a succulent sausage and noodle casserole. Make one or all three!

Tomato Base

1½ cups chopped onion
1½ cups chopped celery
  1 cup shredded carrot
  2 cloves garlic, minced
  3 tablespoons cooking oil
  2 15-ounce cans tomato sauce
  3 6-ounce cans tomato paste

● In a large saucepan cook onion, celery, carrot, and garlic in hot oil till onion is tender but not brown. Stir in tomato sauce and tomato paste. Bring to boiling; reduce heat. Cover and simmer for 15 minutes. Remove from heat; cool. Spoon into three 2½- to 3-cup freezer containers. Seal, label, and freeze.

Packaging the Tomato Base
Dividing the tomato mixture into three portions allows you to pull one container at a time from the freezer. One container of tomato mixture is used in each recipe on the next page. Simply spoon the tomato mixture into three 2½- or 3-cup freezer containers, then seal, label, and freeze.

Manhattan Clam Chowder

1 portion frozen Tomato Base
2 medium potatoes
1½ teaspoons dried thyme, crushed
1 teaspoon sugar
2 6½-ounce cans minced clams, drained

● In a large saucepan combine Tomato Base and 4 cups *water*. Cover and cook over medium-high heat for 10 to 15 minutes or till frozen mixture is thawed; stir occasionally. Meanwhile, peel and chop potatoes. Add potatoes, thyme, sugar, and ¼ teaspoon *salt* to saucepan. Bring to boiling; reduce heat. Cover and simmer for 30 to 35 minutes or till potatoes are tender. Mash potatoes slightly. Stir in clams; heat through. Makes 6 servings.

Spaghetti and Meatballs

Here's another time-saver. Freeze the meatballs ahead of time. When you're ready, just add them to the thawed mixture along with the mushrooms, then cover and simmer 15 minutes.

1 beaten egg
1 cup soft bread crumbs
1 pound lean ground beef
1 portion frozen Tomato Base
2 4-ounce cans sliced mushrooms, drained
⅓ cup dry red wine
2 teaspoons dried oregano, crushed
1 teaspoon sugar
1 teaspoon dried basil, crushed
3 tablespoons all-purpose flour
Hot cooked spaghetti

● In a medium mixing bowl combine egg and 2 tablespoons *water;* stir in crumbs, ¼ teaspoon *salt,* and ⅛ teaspoon *pepper*. Add meat; mix well. With wet hands shape meat mixture into 1-inch meatballs. Place meatballs in a 15x10x1-inch baking pan. Bake in a 375° oven for 20 to 25 minutes or till done. Drain.

● Meanwhile, in a large saucepan combine Tomato Base and 2½ cups *water*. Cover and cook over medium-high heat for 10 to 15 minutes or till thawed, stirring occasionally. Stir in mushrooms, wine, oregano, sugar, and basil. Bring to boiling; reduce heat. Cover and simmer for 15 minutes. Stir together flour and ⅓ cup *water*. Add to mixture in saucepan. Cook and stir till thickened and bubbly, then cook and stir 1 minute more. Stir in meatballs; cover and simmer about 5 minutes or till heated through. Serve over spaghetti. Makes 6 servings.

Sausage-Noodle Casserole

1 portion frozen Tomato Base
1 pound bulk Italian sausage
2 ounces medium noodles
1 10-ounce package frozen peas
1½ cups shredded American cheese (6 ounces)
1 teaspoon chili powder
¾ cup soft bread crumbs
1 tablespoon butter

● In a large saucepan combine Tomato Base and 1 cup *water*. Cover and cook over medium-high heat for 10 to 15 minutes or till thawed, stirring occasionally. Cook meat till brown. Drain off fat. Cook noodles according to package directions; drain.

● Stir noodles, meat, peas, cheese, chili powder, and ⅛ teaspoon *pepper* into mixture in saucepan. Transfer to a 2-quart casserole. Melt butter; toss with crumbs. Sprinkle over casserole. Bake, uncovered, in a 375° oven for 35 to 40 minutes or till heated through. Let stand 5 minutes. Makes 6 servings.

Start with a base...

Look no further for hearty soups and casseroles. Start with Creamy Base, then decide whether to use it in a rich pasta toss, a smooth cheese soup, a chunky clam chowder, or a homey tuna casserole. What a delicious decision to make!

Creamy Base

2 cups nonfat dry milk powder
2 cups water
1 cup chopped onion
2 cloves garlic, minced
¼ cup butter *or* margarine
⅓ cup cornstarch
1 teaspoon salt
½ teaspoon pepper

● In a medium mixing bowl stir together milk powder and water till milk is dissolved. In a medium saucepan cook onion and garlic in butter or margarine till onion is tender. Stir in cornstarch, salt, and pepper. Add milk mixture all at once. Cook and stir till thickened and bubbly, then cook and stir 2 minutes more. Remove from heat. Cool slightly. Pour into two 2-cup freezer containers. Seal, label, and freeze.

Cooking the Creamy Base
After the mixture thickens, be sure to stir it as you continue cooking. Stirring prevents the mixture from sticking to the pan. The additional cooking time is necessary to get the maximum thickening from the cornstarch.

Four-Cheese Pasta and Vegetables

½ cup thinly bias-sliced
    carrots
2 tablespoons butter *or*
    margarine
1 medium green *or* sweet red
    pepper, cut into thin bite-
    size strips
½ cup sliced fresh mushrooms
½ cup sliced zucchini
1 portion frozen Creamy Base
⅔ cup water
⅔ cup milk
⅓ cup shredded Gruyère
    cheese
⅓ cup shredded fontina cheese
⅓ cup shredded mozzarella
    cheese
¼ cup grated Parmesan cheese
5 ounces hot cooked linguine

● In a large saucepan cook the carrots in butter or margarine, covered, over medium heat for 5 minutes. Add green pepper, mushrooms, and zucchini. Cover and cook for 3 to 5 minutes more or till vegetables are crisp-tender, stirring occasionally. Remove vegetables from saucepan.

● In the same saucepan combine the Creamy Base and water. Cover and cook over medium heat about 15 minutes or till thawed, stirring occasionally. Add milk. Cook and stir till heated through. Stir with a wire whisk or beat with a rotary beater till mixture is smooth. Add Gruyère, fontina, mozzarella, and Parmesan cheeses. Cook and stir till cheeses melt. Stir in vegetables; heat through. To serve, toss cheese-vegetable mixture with hot linguine. Makes 5 servings.

Beer-Cheese Soup

Get rid of the lumps in the soup by whisking or beating the thickened mixture before adding the cheese and ham.

1 portion frozen Creamy Base
1¼ cups beer
¾ cup water
1½ cups shredded American
    cheese (6 ounces)
1 cup finely chopped fully
    cooked ham

● In a large saucepan combine Creamy Base, beer, and water. Cover and cook over medium heat about 15 minutes or till frozen mixture is thawed, stirring occasionally.

● Cover and cook about 5 minutes more or till mixture is heated through. Stir with a wire whisk or beat with a rotary beater till smooth. Add cheese and ham; stir till cheese melts. Spoon into soup bowls. Makes 4 or 5 servings.

New England Clam Chowder

2 cups water
1 portion frozen Creamy Base
3 cups cubed cooked potatoes
2 6½-ounce cans minced
   clams, drained
1 cup light cream

● In a large saucepan combine water and Creamy Base. Cover and cook over medium heat about 15 minutes or till frozen mixture is thawed, stirring occasionally. Cover and cook about 5 minutes more or till heated through.

● Stir the base mixture with a wire whisk till smooth. Stir potatoes, clams, and cream into mixture in saucepan. Cover and simmer about 2 minutes more or till heated through. Makes 6 servings.

Tuna-Macaroni Casserole

1 portion frozen Creamy Base
1½ cups water
4 ounces elbow macaroni
   (1 cup)
1 cup shredded American
   cheese (4 ounces)
1 cup frozen peas and carrots
½ teaspoon dry mustard
1 6½-ounce can tuna,
   drained and flaked
¼ cup fine dry bread crumbs
1 tablespoon butter *or*
   margarine, melted
½ teaspoon paprika

● In a large saucepan combine Creamy Base and water. Cover and cook over medium heat about 15 minutes or till frozen mixture is thawed, stirring occasionally. Meanwhile, cook macaroni according to package directions; drain.

● Stir the base mixture with a wire whisk till smooth. Stir cheese, peas and carrots, dry mustard, and macaroni into mixture in saucepan. Cook and stir till heated through. Fold in tuna. Spoon into a 2-quart casserole. Toss together crumbs, butter or margarine, and paprika. Sprinkle over casserole. Bake, uncovered, in a 375° oven about 35 minutes or till heated through. Makes 4 or 5 servings.

SIDE DISHES

Side dishes are an esteemed part of any well-rounded meal—whether your choice is a creamy vegetable casserole, a savory rice pilaf, a frosty fruit salad, or a buttery brown-and-serve bread. You can keep several choices waiting in the freezer to come to your rescue when "something is missing" on the menu. Just reheat one while you prepare the rest of your meal.

Timesaving Tips

Here's a gold mine of handy freezing information to help you save time and serve the best tasting food.

● Many vegetable dishes, such as the Vegetables Au Gratin on page 69, contain cheese. To save time, shred the cheese in advance and freeze it in a freezer container or bag.

● Vegetables used in frozen casseroles should be slightly undercooked. They'll finish cooking when the food is reheated.

● Freeze buttered bread or cracker crumbs separately to add to the top of a casserole during baking.

● Using your blender or food processor, make a batch of bread crumbs with leftover bread. Store the bread crumbs in a freezer container or bag.

● Freeze coffee cakes and sweet rolls unfrosted. After thawing and heating, drizzle with desired frosting.

● Make quick breads in small loaf pans. Not only do you save baking time, but you can freeze them and thaw only as many loaves as you need.

Homemade Frozen Bread Dough

Mix, knead, and freeze! That's all there is to making your own frozen bread dough. You'll find the steps in recipes for Whole Wheat Butterhorns and Cheese Bread Braids on pages 72 and 73. To adapt your own recipes, see these steps that are highlighted below.

● Follow the bread recipe through the mixing and kneading stages.

● Form dough into a ball(s) and freeze. If dough rises before freezing, the bread might have an off-flavor.

● Freeze small amounts of dough for even thawing.

● To use, thaw the dough for 2 to 3 hours at room temperature or overnight in the refrigerator.

● After the dough is thawed, shape as desired.

● For the best volume, let the dough rise till it's slightly more than doubled in size. This can take from 45 minutes to 3½ hours.

● Bake the dough according to recipe directions.

How Long Will It Keep?

To keep a frozen side dish at its freshest, freeze it no longer than recommended. As a general guide, freeze vegetable dishes in this chapter for three to six months and yeast breads for four to eight months.

Mexicali Vegetables

For stove-top reheating, freeze the mixture in a 1-quart freezer container. Transfer the frozen mixture to a saucepan; cover and cook over medium-low heat about 50 minutes.

1 cup vegetable juice cocktail
1 tablespoon quick-cooking tapioca, ground (see tip, page 14)
¼ cup sliced green onion
⅛ teaspoon ground cumin
⅛ teaspoon chili powder
1 10-ounce package frozen whole kernel corn
1 8-ounce can red kidney beans, drained
1 4-ounce can diced green chili peppers, drained
2 tablespoons chopped pimiento

● In a medium saucepan stir together vegetable juice cocktail and tapioca. Add onion, cumin, and chili powder. Cook and stir over medium heat till thickened and bubbly, then cook and stir 2 minutes more. Stir in corn, beans, chili peppers, and pimiento. Cool. Spoon into a 1-quart casserole. Seal, label, and freeze.

● **To serve,** bake the frozen casserole, covered, in a 375° oven about 1¼ hours or till heated through, stirring occasionally. Makes 6 servings.

Wild Rice Pilaf

Keep this sophisticated side dish in mind when company is coming.

¼ cup wild rice
1 cup sliced fresh mushrooms
1 small onion, chopped
1 tablespoon butter *or* margarine
½ cup brown rice
½ cup shredded carrot
2 tablespoons snipped parsley
½ teaspoon dried basil, crushed
1¾ cups chicken broth
¼ cup slivered almonds, toasted

● Run cold water over *uncooked* wild rice in a strainer for 1 minute, lifting rice with fingers to rinse well. In a medium saucepan cook mushrooms and onion in butter or margarine till tender. Stir in wild rice, brown rice, carrot, parsley, and basil. Add chicken broth. Bring to boiling; reduce heat.

● Cover and simmer for 35 to 40 minutes or till brown rice is tender. (The wild rice will be underdone and there should be some liquid left in saucepan.) Spoon rice mixture and any remaining liquid into a 1-quart casserole. Seal, label, and freeze.

● **To serve,** bake the frozen casserole, covered, in a 375° oven for 1 to 1¼ hours or till heated through, stirring occasionally. Sprinkle with almonds. Makes 4 servings.

Whole Wheat Butterhorns
(see recipe, page 72)

Brown-and-Serve Honey Brioche
(see recipe, page 74)

Vegetables Au Gratin

Vegetables Au Gratin

You can substitute fresh broccoli flowerets for the frozen vegetables. Just steam the broccoli for 7 to 10 minutes or till crisp-tender.

1 16-ounce package loose-pack frozen mixed broccoli, green beans, onions, and red peppers
1 cup milk
2 tablespoons cornstarch
¼ teaspoon salt
⅛ teaspoon pepper
1½ cups shredded American cheese (6 ounces)
⅓ cup fine dry bread crumbs
1 tablespoon butter *or* margarine, melted

● Cook vegetables according to package directions; drain. Meanwhile, in a medium saucepan combine milk, cornstarch, salt, and pepper. Cook and stir over medium heat till thickened and bubbly, then cook and stir 2 minutes more. Stir in cheese till it melts; remove from heat. Stir in vegetables. Pour into a 1½-quart casserole. Seal, label, and freeze.

● **To serve,** bake frozen casserole, covered, in a 375° oven for 60 to 65 minutes or till nearly heated through, stirring once.

● In a small mixing bowl combine bread crumbs and butter or margarine; toss to coat. Sprinkle buttered crumbs over vegetable mixture. Bake, uncovered, for 5 to 10 minutes more or till crumbs are golden brown. Makes 6 servings.

Baked Harvest Squash

161 CALORIES SERVING

You can use one 12-ounce package frozen winter squash instead of the fresh. Cook the frozen squash according to package directions.

1¼ to 1½ pounds winter squash
1 large apple, peeled, cored, and chopped
2 tablespoons finely chopped onion
2 tablespoons butter *or* margarine
1 tablespoon brown sugar
½ teaspoon ground cinnamon
¼ teaspoon salt
⅛ teaspoon ground nutmeg
2 tablespoons chopped pecans

● Halve squash and remove seeds and strings. Place halves, cut side down, in a large kettle or Dutch oven. Add water to a depth of 1 inch. Bring to boiling; reduce heat. Cover and simmer for 35 to 40 minutes or till tender; drain. Remove pulp from shells; mash pulp (should have 1½ cups mashed squash).

● In a large saucepan or skillet cook apple and onion in butter or margarine, covered, till onion is tender, stirring occasionally. Stir in squash, brown sugar, cinnamon, salt, and nutmeg. Spoon into a 2½- to 3-cup casserole. Seal, label, and freeze.

● **To serve,** bake frozen casserole, covered, in a 375° oven about 1¼ hours or till heated through, stirring once. Sprinkle with nuts before serving. Makes 4 servings.

Duchess Potatoes

If you don't have a pastry bag and tip for piping the potatoes, just spoon them into mounds.

1½ **cups cooked and mashed**
    potatoes
1 **to 2 tablespoons light cream**
    or **milk**
2 **tablespoons butter** *or*
    margarine
1 **egg**
¼ **teaspoon salt**
    Several dashes ground
      nutmeg
    Dash pepper
2 **tablespoons butter** *or*
    margarine, melted

● In a large mixing bowl or a small mixer bowl, combine warm potatoes, cream or milk, 2 tablespoons butter or margarine, egg, salt, nutmeg, and pepper. Mash with a potato masher or beat with an electric mixer on low speed till smooth.

● Line a baking sheet with waxed paper. Using a pastry bag with a large star tip, pipe potato mixture into 6 mounds onto baking sheet. Freeze about 45 minutes or till firm. Remove potato mounds from baking sheet and transfer to a freezer container or bag. Seal, label, and freeze.

● **To serve,** place frozen potato mounds on a greased baking sheet. Brush with 2 tablespoons melted butter or margarine. Bake, uncovered, in a 375° oven for 20 to 25 minutes or till heated through. Makes 6 servings.

Piping the potatoes
Carefully spoon the potato mixture into a pastry bag fitted with a large open-star writing tip. Fold the bag and hold it closed with your writing hand. Support the filled pastry bag with your other hand.

To pipe the mixture, hold the filled bag perpendicular to the baking sheet. Then force the potato mixture through the tip by squeezing the end of the bag with your writing hand.

Spinach-Stuffed Spuds

Serve this with a juicy burger and you've got a great meal.

4 medium baking potatoes
  (1¼ to 1½ pounds total)
1 10-ounce package frozen
  chopped spinach
2 tablespoons butter *or*
  margarine
½ cup shredded cheddar
  cheese (2 ounces)
½ cup sour cream dip with
  onion
¼ teaspoon pepper
  Shredded cheddar cheese
  (optional)

● Scrub potatoes thoroughly and prick with a fork. Bake in a 425° oven for 45 to 60 minutes or till done. Meanwhile, cook spinach according to package directions. Drain well; squeeze out excess liquid.

● Cut a lengthwise slice from the top of each potato. Discard skin from slice. Scoop out insides of potatoes, leaving ¼-inch shells. Set shells aside. Add potato portions from top slices to potatoes scooped from insides; mash.

● Add butter or margarine to potatoes; mash. Stir in ½ cup cheese, sour cream dip, pepper, and spinach till well combined. Spoon mixture into the reserved potato shells. Wrap each potato in heavy-duty foil or place potatoes in a freezer container. Seal, label, and freeze.

● **To serve,** unwrap frozen potatoes; transfer to a baking sheet. Bake in a 375° oven about 45 minutes or till heated through. Sprinkle with more cheese, if desired. Makes 4 servings.

Strawberry-Pineapple Salads

Oooh! Wake up your palate with these fruity frozen delights.

1 3-ounce package cream
  cheese, softened
1 8-ounce carton strawberry
  yogurt
2 tablespoons sugar
1 8¼-ounce can crushed
  pineapple, drained
¼ cup chopped celery
  Lettuce leaves
¼ cup dairy sour cream
6 fresh whole strawberries
  (optional)

● In a small mixer bowl beat cream cheese till fluffy. Beat in yogurt and sugar till smooth. Stir in pineapple and celery. Line 6 muffin cups with paper bake cups. Spoon about ⅓ cup yogurt mixture into each cup.

● Freeze the filled cups for 2 to 2½ hours or till firm, then transfer to a freezer bag. Seal, label, and freeze.

● **To serve,** peel off paper bake cups. Arrange frozen yogurt cups on 6 lettuce-lined salad plates. Let stand for 20 minutes before serving. Dollop each serving with sour cream and top with a strawberry, if desired. Makes 6 servings.

Whole Wheat Butterhorns

Create buttery whole-grain rolls from homemade frozen bread dough. (Pictured on page 68.)

2½ to 3 cups all-purpose flour
  2 packages active dry yeast
1¾ cups water
  ⅓ cup packed brown sugar
  3 tablespoons shortening
  ½ teaspoon salt
  2 cups whole wheat flour
  6 tablespoons butter *or*
     margarine, softened
     Butter *or* margarine, melted

● In a large mixer bowl stir together *1½ cups* of all-purpose flour and yeast. In a small saucepan heat water, sugar, shortening, and salt just till warm (115° to 120°) and shortening is almost melted, stirring constantly. Add to flour mixture.

● Beat with an electric mixer on low speed for 30 seconds, scraping the sides of the bowl. Beat for 3 minutes on high speed. With a spoon, stir in whole wheat flour and as much all-purpose flour as you can.

● Turn out onto a lightly floured surface. Knead in enough remaining all-purpose flour to make a moderately stiff dough that is smooth and elastic (6 to 8 minutes total).

● Divide dough into thirds. Form each portion into a smooth ball. Wrap each ball in clear plastic wrap and transfer to freezer bags. Seal, label, and freeze.

● **To serve,** let dough stand in freezer bags at room temperature about 2½ hours or till thawed (or thaw overnight in the refrigerator). On a lightly floured surface roll 1 ball of dough into a 12-inch circle; spread with *2 tablespoons* of the softened butter or margarine. Cut circle into 12 wedges.

● To shape the rolls, begin at the wide end of the wedge and roll dough toward the point. Place, point side down, 2 to 3 inches apart on a greased baking sheet. Repeat with remaining dough. Cover and let the rolls rise in a warm place till slightly more than doubled (about 45 minutes). Brush with melted butter.

● Bake in a 400° oven for 10 to 12 minutes or till brown. Remove from baking sheet; cool on wire racks. Brush again with melted butter or margarine. Makes 36 rolls.

Cheese Bread Braids

Bring the cheese to room temperature so it will work into the dough easily.

6¾ to 7¼ cups all-purpose flour
2 packages active dry yeast
2 cups milk
¼ cup sugar
¼ cup butter *or* margarine
1 teaspoon salt
3 eggs
2 cups shredded cheddar cheese (8 ounces)

● Combine *3 cups* flour and yeast. Heat milk, sugar, butter, and salt just till warm (115° to 120°) and butter is almost melted, stirring constantly. Add to flour mixture. Add eggs and cheese. Beat with an electric mixer on low speed for 30 seconds, scraping bowl. Beat for 3 minutes on high speed. Using a spoon, stir in as much flour as you can. Turn out onto a lightly floured surface. Knead in enough remaining flour to make a moderately stiff dough that is smooth and elastic (6 to 8 minutes total). Divide into thirds. Form each portion into a ball. Wrap in clear plastic wrap; transfer to freezer bags. Seal, label, and freeze.

● **To serve,** let dough stand in freezer bags at room temperature about 2½ hours or till thawed (or thaw overnight in refrigerator). Divide each ball into 3 portions. Roll portions into 15-inch ropes. Line up 3 ropes on a greased baking sheet. Braid loosely. Pinch ends; tuck under. Repeat with remaining dough. Cover; let rise till slightly more than doubled (about 1 hour). Bake in a 375° oven about 20 minutes or till brown. Cool. Makes 3 braids.

Braiding the dough

Roll each portion of dough into a 15-inch-long rope. Place three ropes 1 inch apart on a greased baking sheet. Braid loosely, beginning in the middle and working toward the ends. Pinch the ends together and tuck under braid.

Braiding loosely gives the dough room to expand without cracking or losing its shape. Beginning in the middle helps prevent stretching of the dough, which would make the braid uneven.

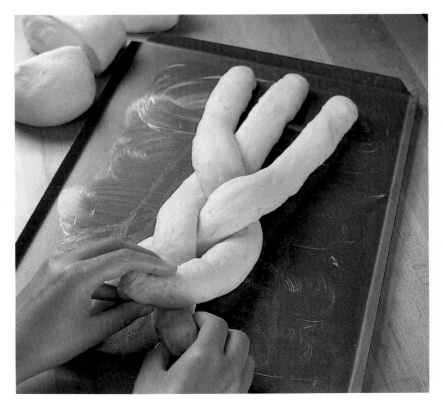

Brown-and-Serve Honey Brioche

A rich French yeast bread that's shaped like a fat bun with a topknot. (Pictured on page 68.)

1 package active dry yeast
¼ cup warm water (110° to 115°)
½ cup butter *or* margarine
¼ cup honey
½ teaspoon salt
4 cups all-purpose flour
⅓ cup milk
3 eggs
1 tablespoon poppy seed
Milk

● Soften yeast in warm water. In a large mixer bowl beat together butter or margarine, honey, and salt. Add *1 cup* of the flour and ⅓ cup milk. Stir till well combined.

● Beat in eggs. Add softened yeast; beat well. Stir in remaining flour and poppy seed till smooth. Transfer to a greased bowl. Cover and let rise in a warm place till double (about 2 hours). Refrigerate for 4 hours or overnight.

● Punch down dough. Turn out onto a lightly floured surface; divide into quarters. Set 1 portion aside. Divide each of the remaining portions into 6 pieces, making a total of 18.

● With lightly floured hands, form each piece into a ball, tucking under edges. Place each ball in a greased muffin cup. Divide reserved dough into 18 pieces; shape into balls.

● With a floured finger, make an indentation in each large ball in the muffin cups. Press a small ball into each indentation. Cover and let rise till nearly double (30 to 40 minutes). Bake in a 325° oven for 10 to 12 minutes. *Do not brown.* Remove from pans and cool. Transfer to freezer bags. Seal, label, and freeze.

● **To serve,** partially uncover rolls. Let stand at room temperature for 15 minutes. Uncover completely; place on a greased baking sheet. Brush with a little milk. Bake in a 375° oven for 10 to 12 minutes or till brown. Cool. Makes 18 rolls.

Spicy Garlic Bread

For fewer servings, cut the loaf of French bread in half and freeze portions separately.

1 7- to 8-ounce loaf unsliced French bread
3 tablespoons butter *or* margarine, softened
⅛ teaspoon garlic powder
Dash ground red pepper
3 tablespoons grated Parmesan cheese

● Cut bread into 1-inch slices, cutting to, but not through, the bottom crust. Stir together butter or margarine, garlic powder, and red pepper. Spread mixture between slices; sprinkle cheese between slices. Seal in heavy-duty foil, label, and freeze.

● **To serve,** bake the frozen bread, wrapped in foil, in a 375° oven about 25 minutes or till the loaf is heated through. Makes 12 to 14 servings.

DESSERTS

What a treat! By freezing dessert ahead, you can forget about the last-minute rush at mealtime and enjoy dessert just as much as everyone else does. Are you craving a fruity dessert? Try your hand at Fresh Cherry Pie. If you're in a bit of a hurry, whip up Quick Crème de Menthe Pie. Or when the gang deserves a special indulgence, bring on Mocha-Rum Cheesecake.

Dessert Do-Aheads

With a little planning, you can stock your freezer with delightful desserts or a few simple garnishes to use at a moment's notice.

To save last-minute scurrying, scoop servings of ice cream or sherbet into individual dessert dishes or bowls and freeze. Make sure the dishes can withstand the cold freezer air. Or you can place individual scoops on a baking sheet lined with waxed paper. Freeze till firm, then transfer scoops to a freezer container. When it's time for dessert, simply remove the scoops from the container and place them in dishes or on top of warm fruit-pie slices.

To avoid having to whip cream at the last minute, whip it several days in advance and spoon it into mounds on a baking sheet lined with waxed paper. Freeze till firm, then transfer mounds to a freezer container. To serve, place a mound on each serving of dessert. Let dessert stand at room temperature for 20 to 30 minutes or till whipped cream is thawed.

Homemade Frozen Pie Shells

Save yourself last-minute preparation time by freezing pastry shells. Simply make your favorite pastry or use the recipe on page 77. Then line a pie plate with the pastry, or stack the rolled-out pastry between layers of waxed paper, or bake the pastry in a pie plate and completely cool. Then seal in moisture- and vaporproof wrap, label, and freeze for up to two months.

When you're ready to use the frozen unbaked pastry shell, bake as you would an unfrozen shell. To use the frozen stack of rolled-out pastry, let it stand at room temperature about 30 minutes or till thawed. Then line a pie plate(s) with the pastry and bake as usual. Use the frozen baked pie shell as you would a freshly baked and cooled pie shell.

How Long Will It Keep?

Your dessert may lose its sweet appeal if you store it in the freezer too long. As a general guide, you can store cakes in the freezer for six months, unbaked cookies for six months, baked cookies for six to twelve months, and unbaked pies for three months.

Quick Crème de Menthe Pie

Set the pie plate on a warm, damp towel about 5 minutes before serving to help loosen the crumb crust from the bottom.

25 chocolate wafers, crushed (1⅓ cups)
6 tablespoons butter *or* margarine, melted
1 7-ounce jar marshmallow creme
¼ cup green crème de menthe
½ cup finely chopped layered chocolate-mint candies (16 rectangles)
2 cups whipping cream

● In a mixing bowl toss together crushed wafers and butter or margarine till well combined. Press crumb mixture firmly onto bottom and up the sides of a 9-inch pie plate; set aside. In a large mixer bowl beat marshmallow creme and crème de menthe with an electric mixer till smooth. Fold in candy. In a small mixer bowl beat whipping cream till soft peaks form (tips curl). Fold into marshmallow mixture. Spoon into the crumb crust. Freeze, uncovered, for 1 to 2 hours or till firm. Remove from freezer. Seal, label, and freeze.

● **To serve,** unwrap frozen pie. Set the pie plate on a warm, damp towel. Makes 8 servings.

Fresh Cherry Pie

4 cups fresh *or* frozen unsweetened pitted tart red cherries (20 ounces)
1 cup sugar
½ cup water
3 tablespoons quick-cooking tapioca
1 tablespoon cherry brandy *or* orange juice
Pastry for Double-Crust Pie
1 tablespoon butter *or* margarine

● In a large mixing bowl combine fresh or frozen cherries, sugar, water, tapioca, and brandy. Let stand 30 minutes, stirring occasionally. Meanwhile, prepare pastry. Spoon cherry mixture into pastry-lined pie plate; dot with butter. Adjust top crust; trim to ½ inch beyond edge. Seal and flute edge high. Cover pie with an inverted 10-inch paper plate. Seal, label, and freeze.

● **To serve,** unwrap frozen pie. Cut slits in top crust. Bake in a 400° oven about 65 minutes or till crust is golden brown. Makes 8 servings.

Pastry for Double-Crust Pie: In a mixing bowl stir together 2 cups all-purpose *flour* and ½ teaspoon *salt.* Cut in ⅔ cup *shortening* or *lard* till pieces are the size of small peas. Sprinkle 1 tablespoon cold *water* over part of the mixture; gently toss with a fork. Push to side of bowl. Repeat till all is moistened (use 6 to 7 tablespoons cold water total).

Divide dough in half. For bottom crust, on a lightly floured surface roll half of the dough into a 12-inch circle; fit into a 9-inch pie plate. Trim pastry even with the rim. For top crust, roll remaining dough into a 12-inch circle. *Do not* cut slits in dough.

Fresh Apple Pie: Prepare Fresh Cherry Pie as directed, *except* substitute 6 cups peeled and sliced *cooking apples* for the cherries, reduce the sugar to ¾ *cup,* omit the water and tapioca, and substitute 1 tablespoon *lemon juice* for the brandy or orange juice. Stir ½ teaspoon ground *cinnamon* into the apple mixture; omit the standing time. Continue as directed in the recipe.

Mocha-Rum Cheesecake

Absolutely the tops in sinfulness!

1½ cups finely crushed crisp oatmeal cookies (12 to 14 cookies)
¼ cup butter *or* margarine, melted
¼ cup rum
1 tablespoon instant coffee crystals
3 8-ounce packages cream cheese, softened
1 cup sugar
4 squares (4 ounces) semisweet chocolate, melted and cooled
2 tablespoons all-purpose flour
1 teaspoon vanilla
3 eggs
  Whipped cream (optional)
  Chocolate curls (optional)
  Fresh *or* frozen-and-thawed raspberries (optional)
  Fresh mint leaves (optional)

● In a mixing bowl toss together crushed cookies and butter or margarine till well combined. Press onto the bottom and 1½ inches up the sides of a 9-inch springform pan.

● Stir together rum and coffee crystals. In a large mixer bowl beat cream cheese, sugar, chocolate, flour, and vanilla just till combined. Add eggs all at once. Beat just till combined. *Do not overbeat.* Stir in rum mixture. Pour mixture into crumb crust.

● Bake in a 350° oven for 50 to 60 minutes or till center appears to be set; cool for 10 minutes. With a knife or small metal spatula loosen sides of cheesecake from pan; remove sides of pan. Let cheesecake stand at room temperature about 2 hours or till cool. Freeze, uncovered, about 1 hour or till firm. Remove bottom of pan. Transfer cheesecake to a large freezer bag or container. Seal, label, and freeze.

● **To serve,** thaw cheesecake, loosely covered, for 24 hours in the refrigerator. Garnish with whipped cream, chocolate curls, raspberries, and mint leaves, if desired. Makes 12 servings.

Individual Praline Cheesecakes

Look for packages of graham cracker tart shells near the baking supplies at the grocery store.

1 8-ounce package cream cheese, softened
½ cup packed brown sugar
1 teaspoon vanilla
2 eggs
1½ cups dairy sour cream
12 graham cracker tart shells
36 pecan halves

● In a small mixer bowl beat cream cheese till smooth. Add sugar and vanilla; beat till well combined. Add eggs all at once. Beat just till combined. *Do not overbeat.* Stir in sour cream.

● Pour mixture into tart shells. Bake in a 350° oven for 15 to 18 minutes or till center appears set; cool. Place 3 pecan halves on top of each cheesecake in a spokelike fashion. Freeze, uncovered, about 1 hour or till firm. Transfer to a freezer container or bags. Seal, label, and freeze.

● **To serve,** thaw the cheesecakes, loosely covered, about 2 hours at room temperature or overnight in the refrigerator. Makes 12 servings.

Mocha-Rum Cheesecake

Berries 'n' Cream Torte

If you're in a hurry, replace the frozen filling with 1 quart of your favorite ice cream.

1 14-ounce can (1¼ cups)
    sweetened condensed
    milk
⅓ cup lemon juice
1 pint fresh strawberries,
    mashed (1⅓ cups)
1 cup whipping cream
½ cup coarsely chopped
    almonds, toasted
1 11-ounce package 3-inch
    soft apple spice *or*
    oatmeal cookies
3 tablespoons sugar
2 teaspoons cornstarch
½ cup unsweetened pineapple
    juice
1 tablespoon brandy
    (optional)
2 cups desired berries

● For strawberry filling, in a mixing bowl combine sweetened condensed milk and lemon juice; stir just till mixture begins to thicken. Stir mashed strawberries into milk mixture. Beat whipping cream just till it mounds; fold into berry mixture. Cover and freeze till firm. Break up frozen mixture and place in a chilled mixer bowl; beat with an electric mixer till smooth. Fold in chopped almonds.

● For the torte, line a 2-quart soufflé dish with clear plastic wrap, extending wrap 2 to 3 inches above dish. Gently press 7 or 8 cookies around the inside of dish, overlapping to form a scalloped edge. Place about *half* of the remaining cookies on the bottom of dish, breaking cookies as necessary to fit.

● Spoon *half* of the strawberry filling over cookies in bottom of dish. Arrange remaining cookies on top. Spoon on the remaining strawberry filling. Seal, label, and freeze.

● **To serve,** for sauce, in a small saucepan combine sugar and cornstarch. Stir in pineapple juice. Cook and stir till thickened and bubbly, then cook and stir 2 minutes more. Remove from heat; stir in brandy. Cover surface with clear plastic wrap. Cool.

● Remove frozen torte from dish by pulling up on plastic wrap; carefully remove plastic wrap. Transfer torte to a serving platter. Top with desired berries; spoon sauce over the berries. Makes 8 to 10 servings.

1 Assembling the ice cream torte

After lining the dish with plastic wrap, press 7 or 8 cookies around the inside of the dish. Overlap the cookies in the dish to form a scalloped edge. Place half of the remaining cookies in the bottom of the dish. You might have to break some of the cookies to fit. Spoon half of the strawberry filling over the cookies in the bottom of the dish and arrange the remaining cookies on top. Then top with the remaining strawberry filling.

2 Serving the ice cream torte

After removing the frozen torte from the soufflé dish and discarding the plastic wrap, arrange desired berries on top. Carefully spoon the sauce over the berries, letting some of the sauce run down the sides of the torte.

If fresh berries are not available, use frozen fruit instead. Thaw and drain the frozen fruit before placing it on the torte.

Pumpkin Cake Roll

¾ cup all-purpose flour
2 teaspoons ground cinnamon
1 teaspoon baking powder
1 teaspoon ground ginger
½ teaspoon ground nutmeg
¼ teaspoon salt
3 eggs
1 cup sugar
⅔ cup canned pumpkin
1 cup chopped walnuts
  Sifted powdered sugar
1 quart rum raisin *or* vanilla
  ice cream
½ cup canned vanilla frosting
  Chopped walnuts

● Grease and lightly flour a 15x10x1-inch baking pan. Stir together flour, cinnamon, baking powder, ginger, nutmeg, and salt. In a large mixer bowl beat eggs with an electric mixer on high speed about 5 minutes or till thick and lemon colored. Gradually add sugar, beating 5 minutes more. Stir in pumpkin. Fold dry ingredients into pumpkin mixture. Spread evenly in prepared pan. Sprinkle with 1 cup chopped walnuts. Bake in a 375° oven for 12 to 15 minutes or till cake springs back and shows no imprint when lightly touched.

● Immediately loosen edges of cake from pan and turn out onto a towel sprinkled with powdered sugar. Starting at narrow end, loosely roll warm cake and the towel (the nuts should be on the outside of the roll). Cool, seam side down, on a wire rack. Stir ice cream to soften. Unroll cake; spread with ice cream to within 1 inch of the edges. Roll up cake and ice cream. Place on a baking sheet and freeze about 1 hour or till firm. Wrap cake roll in heavy-duty foil, label, and freeze.

● **To serve,** unwrap cake roll and place on a serving platter. In a small saucepan heat frosting over low heat for 1 to 2 minutes or till of drizzling consistency, stirring frequently. Spoon over cake roll, allowing frosting to drizzle down sides. Sprinkle additional nuts down center. Slice to serve. Makes 10 servings.

Piña Colada Soufflés

As airy as a tropical breeze.

183 CALORIES SERVING

2 tablespoons butter *or*
  margarine
3 tablespoons all-purpose
  flour
⅓ cup milk
⅓ cup unsweetened pineapple
  juice
2 egg yolks
¼ teaspoon rum flavoring
2 egg whites
2 tablespoons sugar
⅓ cup flaked coconut
  Sifted powdered sugar

● For soufflés, in a small saucepan melt butter or margarine; stir in flour. Add milk. Cook and stir till the mixture forms a ball; remove from heat. Gradually stir in pineapple juice.

● In a small mixer bowl beat egg yolks with an electric mixer about 4 minutes or till thick and lemon colored. Gradually beat in the pineapple mixture and rum flavoring. Wash the beaters thoroughly. Beat egg whites till soft peaks form (tips curl). Gradually add sugar, beating till stiff peaks form (tips stand straight). Fold in pineapple mixture and coconut. Spoon into four 6-ounce custard cups. Seal, label, and freeze.

● **To serve,** unwrap frozen soufflés and place in a 9x9x2-inch baking pan. Pour *boiling water* into pan around cups to a depth of ½ inch. Bake, uncovered, in a 375° oven for 35 to 40 minutes or till a knife inserted near center comes out clean. Sprinkle with powdered sugar; serve immediately. Makes 4 servings.

Piña Colada Soufflés

Chocolate Layered Trifle

Luscious layers of tender cake, coffee liqueur, chocolate pudding, and whipped cream.

⅔ cup sugar
2 tablespoons cornstarch
2 cups milk
2 squares (2 ounces) unsweetened chocolate, chopped
2 beaten egg yolks
2 tablespoons butter *or*
   margarine
2 teaspoons vanilla
3 cups angel cake cubes
3 tablespoons coffee liqueur
1½ cups whipping cream,
   whipped
   Fresh fruit (optional)

● For pudding, in a heavy medium saucepan combine sugar and cornstarch. Stir in milk and chocolate. Cook and stir till thickened and bubbly, then cook and stir 2 minutes more.

● Gradually stir about *1 cup* of the hot mixture into egg yolks. Return all to saucepan. Cook and stir 2 minutes more. Remove from heat. Stir in butter or margarine and vanilla. Cover surface with clear plastic wrap; chill without stirring.

● To assemble, place *1 cup* of the cake cubes in the bottom of a 1½-quart tempered soufflé dish or 2-quart glass bowl or casse-role. Sprinkle with *1 tablespoon* of the liqueur. Spread *one-third* of the pudding over cake mixture. Spread with *one-third* of the whipped cream. Repeat layers twice, ending with the whipped cream. Seal, label, and freeze.

● **To serve,** thaw frozen trifle for 24 hours in the refrigerator. Garnish with fresh fruit, if desired. Makes 6 servings.

Double Chocolate-Nut Slices

1 3-ounce package cream
   cheese, softened
⅓ cup sugar
1 teaspoon vanilla
½ cup miniature semisweet
   chocolate pieces *or*
   semisweet chocolate
   pieces, chopped
½ cup finely chopped nuts
¼ cup finely crushed graham
   crackers *or* vanilla wafers
1½ cups all-purpose flour
½ teaspoon baking soda
¼ teaspoon salt
⅓ cup butter *or* margarine
1 cup sifted powdered sugar
2 squares (2 ounces) unsweetened chocolate, melted
1 egg
1 teaspoon vanilla

● For filling, in a small mixer bowl beat cream cheese, sugar, and 1 teaspoon vanilla with an electric mixer till smooth. Stir in semisweet pieces, nuts, and crumbs. Cover and chill.

● For the dough, in a small bowl stir together flour, soda, and salt. In a large mixer bowl beat butter or margarine with an electric mixer on medium speed for 30 seconds. Add powdered sugar, beating till well combined. Beat in melted chocolate, egg, and 1 teaspoon vanilla. Add dry ingredients, beating till well combined (mixture will be stiff). Cover and chill for 30 minutes.

● Roll the dough between 2 pieces of waxed paper into a 14x4½-inch rectangle. Remove the top piece of waxed paper. Shape the cream cheese mixture into a 14-inch log, then place it on the dough. Roll dough around cream cheese mixture, remov-ing bottom piece of waxed paper. Moisten and seal edges of dough. Seal in moisture- and vaporproof wrap, label, and freeze.

● **To serve,** unwrap frozen dough and cut into about ¼-inch slices. Place slices on a greased cookie sheet. Bake in a 375° oven about 8 minutes or till edges of cookies are firm and slight-ly brown. Cool about 1 minute; remove from cookie sheet. Cool on a wire rack. Makes about 48 cookies.

APPETIZERS

Finger foods, hors d'oeuvres, or nibbles. Whatever you call them, they all mean party! Choose a creamy dip, savory-filled pastries, or saucy meatballs. Although the food is an important part of any celebration, enjoying the party is important, too. So make the food ahead and freeze it. Then at party time you can be where you should be—with your friends!

Scaling Down Servings

Many recipes in this section are just as well suited to small gatherings as large ones. Several recipes make individual items, allowing you to grab and prepare as many nibbles from the freezer as you need.

A good example of this is the Greek-Style Pastries on page 92. This recipe makes a whopping 45 pastries. But even if you're inviting only a few guests, go ahead and make the entire recipe. Then simply bake as many of the frozen pastries as you like. Save the remaining pastries in the freezer for the next time you entertain.

Keeping Drinks Cold

Here are a couple of ways to keep your beverages cold while you're enjoying the appetizers in this chapter.

When you serve punch, add an ice ring to keep it cool and dress it up at the same time. Making an ice ring is as easy as pouring water. Simply fill a ring mold with water or another desired beverage and freeze till firm. For a fruit-filled ice ring, line the bottom of the ring mold with citrus slices, berries, or melon balls. Add enough water to cover the fruit and freeze till firm. Then fill the mold with more water and freeze till firm.

Another great way to keep drinks such as iced tea cold is to freeze the beverages ahead of time in ice cube trays. Your guests can use the cubes to cool their drinks without diluting them. You can even go a step further by placing a small slice of lemon or a fresh berry in each compartment of the tray before you fill it for freezing.

How Long Will It Keep?

If you wait too long to dig your make-ahead appetizers out of the freezer, you'll be disappointed by the flavor and texture. As a general guide, you can store the recipes in this chapter for one month.

Brandied Crab Terrine

Especially elegant if you garnish with parsley sprigs and serve with unsalted crackers.

8 ounces fresh *or* frozen
  whitefish *or* other fish
  fillets
1 6-ounce package frozen
  crabmeat, thawed and
  drained
1 8-ounce package cream
  cheese, softened
¼ cup finely chopped green
  onion
3 tablespoons brandy
1 tablespoon snipped parsley
¼ teaspoon salt
¼ teaspoon dried tarragon,
  crushed
¼ teaspoon pepper
  Lettuce leaves
  Assorted crackers

● Thaw fish, if frozen. Place fish in a medium skillet. Add enough water to almost cover fish. Bring to boiling; reduce heat. Cover and simmer for 4 to 6 minutes or till fish flakes easily with a fork. Drain well.

● In a small mixing bowl combine cooked fish and crabmeat. With a fork, finely flake fish mixture. In a small mixer bowl beat cream cheese till fluffy. Add onion, brandy, parsley, salt, tarragon, and pepper. Beat with an electric mixer on medium speed till well combined. Fold in fish mixture. Spoon into a lightly oiled 7½x3½x2-inch loaf pan. Seal, label, and freeze.

● **To serve,** thaw the frozen fish mixture, covered, in the refrigerator for 24 hours. Unmold onto a lettuce-lined platter. Serve with assorted crackers. Makes 16 servings.

Orange 'n' Honey Meatballs

Meaty little morsels with an Oriental flavor.

1 beaten egg
¼ cup milk
¼ cup fine dry bread crumbs
1 tablespoon snipped parsley
1 teaspoon grated gingerroot
¼ teaspoon salt
⅛ teaspoon pepper
1 pound ground pork
1 cup orange juice
1 tablespoon quick-cooking
  tapioca, ground (see tip,
  page 14)
2 tablespoons butter *or*
  margarine
2 tablespoons dry white wine
2 tablespoons honey
1 tablespoon soy sauce

● For meatballs, in a mixing bowl combine egg and milk. Stir in crumbs, parsley, gingerroot, salt, and pepper. Add meat; mix well. With wet hands shape meat mixture into 1¼-inch meatballs. Arrange in an ungreased 15x10x1-inch baking pan. Bake in a 350° oven for 15 to 20 minutes or till no longer pink. Drain and cool. Place meatballs in a single layer in a baking pan. Freeze about 1 hour or till firm. Transfer meatballs to a freezer container or bag. Seal, label, and freeze.

● For sauce, in a small mixing bowl stir together orange juice and tapioca. In a small saucepan melt butter or margarine. Stir in wine, honey, soy sauce, and orange juice mixture. Cook and stir till thickened and bubbly, then cook and stir 2 minutes more. Cool. Transfer sauce to a 1½- to 2-cup freezer container. Seal, label, and freeze.

● **To serve,** place frozen sauce in a medium saucepan. Cover and cook over low heat for 10 to 15 minutes or till nearly thawed. Add frozen meatballs to sauce. Cover and cook for 30 to 40 minutes or till heated through, stirring occasionally. Makes 36 meatballs.

Smoked Salmon Dip

Smoked Salmon Dip

Thirty seconds—that's all the time it takes to make the garnish pictured. Just reserve a strip of smoked salmon and coil it into the shape of a rose.

6 ounces thinly sliced smoked salmon
2 3-ounce packages cream cheese, softened
¼ cup milk
2 teaspoons lemon juice
1 teaspoon prepared horseradish
⅛ teaspoon pepper
Smoked salmon rose (optional)
Fresh dill (optional)
Assorted fresh vegetable dippers such as steamed asparagus spears, pea pods, broccoli flowerets, and brussels sprouts, and raw cucumber slices and mushrooms

● Finely chop salmon. In a small mixing bowl stir together salmon, cheese, milk, lemon juice, horseradish, and pepper. Transfer to a 2-cup freezer container. Seal, label, and freeze.

● **To serve,** thaw the container of frozen dip for 24 hours in the refrigerator. Stir dip; spoon into a small serving bowl. Garnish with a salmon rose and dill, if desired. Arrange vegetables on a serving platter. Makes 1½ cups dip.

Cheesy Crab Rolls

Crusty bread on the outside, swirls of delicate crab and cheese in the middle.

10 slices bread
¾ cup shredded American cheese (3 ounces)
2 tablespoons butter *or* margarine
1 tablespoon milk *or* dry white wine
1 6-ounce can crabmeat, drained, flaked, and cartilage removed
⅓ cup butter *or* margarine, melted
½ teaspoon paprika

● Trim crusts from bread slices. With a rolling pin, roll out the bread to flatten. In a small saucepan heat cheese and 2 tablespoons butter or margarine over low heat till cheese melts, stirring constantly. Stir in milk or wine till smooth; stir in crabmeat. Spread crab mixture on 1 side of each flattened bread slice; roll up jelly-roll style.

● In a small mixing bowl combine ⅓ cup melted butter or margarine and paprika. Brush butter mixture lightly over crab rolls. Place rolls, seam side down, on a baking sheet lined with waxed paper. Freeze, uncovered, about 1 hour or till firm. Transfer to a freezer container or bags. Seal, label, and freeze.

● **To serve,** unwrap frozen crab rolls and let stand at room temperature for 10 minutes. Cut each roll into 4 slices. Arrange slices on a greased baking sheet. Bake, uncovered, in a 375° oven about 12 minutes or till bread is golden brown and crisp. Makes 40 crab rolls.

Dill-Cheese Puffs

Our staff likes to call these "puddle-ups." And you'll know why once you see how the cheese pools at the bottom of the bread cubes after they're dipped.

1 cup shredded cheddar
   cheese (4 ounces)
1 3-ounce package cream
   cheese with chives, cubed
¼ cup butter *or* margarine
1 teaspoon dried dillweed
2 egg whites
24 to 30 1-inch cubes French
   bread *or* firm-textured rye
   bread

● In a medium saucepan combine cheddar cheese, cream cheese, butter or margarine, and dillweed. Heat and stir over low heat till cheeses melt; remove from heat.

● In a small mixer bowl beat egg whites with an electric mixer on high speed till stiff peaks form (tips stand straight). Fold cheese mixture into beaten egg whites.

● Line a baking sheet with waxed paper. Dip bread cubes into cheese-egg white mixture, gently scraping off excess. Place coated bread cubes on the baking sheet. Freeze, uncovered, for 30 to 60 minutes or till firm. Transfer bread cubes to a freezer container or bags. Seal, label, and freeze.

● **To serve,** place frozen bread cubes on a lightly greased baking sheet. Bake, uncovered, in a 425° oven for 10 to 12 minutes or till golden brown. Serve warm. Makes 24 to 30 puffs.

Dipping the bread cubes
Use a long-tined fork or a skewer to spear the bread cubes one at a time. Dip the cubes into the cheese-egg white mixture, gently scraping off excess. Then place the coated bread cubes on a baking sheet lined with waxed paper.

When you're ready to heat the frozen bread cubes, place them on a baking sheet, "puddle side" up. This way the puddle of cheese-egg white mixture will soften and even out during baking.

Pastry Twists

A double-duty recipe! You can nibble on these as a snack or serve them with a bowl of hot soup. (Pictured on page 40.)

1 cup all-purpose flour
2 tablespoons grated
    Parmesan cheese
1 teaspoon caraway seed
½ cup butter *or* margarine
1 cup shredded cheddar
    cheese (4 ounces)
2 to 3 tablespoons cold beer
    or water
    Beer *or* milk
    Sesame *or* poppy seed
    (optional)

● In a medium mixing bowl stir together flour, Parmesan cheese, and caraway seed. Cut in butter or margarine till pieces are the size of small peas. Stir in cheddar cheese.

● Sprinkle *1 tablespoon* of the beer or water over part of the dry mixture; gently toss with a fork. Push to side of bowl. Repeat till all is moistened.

● Form the dough into a ball; flatten ball of dough with your hands. Divide in half, then divide each half into 12 portions, making 24 portions total. On a lightly floured surface roll each portion of dough into a rope 11 inches long.

● To shape each twist, cut a rope in half. Pinch ends together; twist the 2 halves together. Tuck ends under. Place on an ungreased baking sheet. Brush lightly with additional beer or milk; sprinkle with sesame or poppy seed, if desired. Repeat with remaining ropes of dough.

● Bake in a 425° oven for 10 to 12 minutes or till golden brown. Remove and cool on wire racks. Transfer to a freezer container or bags. Seal, label, and freeze.

● **To serve,** place frozen pastry twists on an ungreased baking sheet. Bake in a 350° oven for 5 to 7 minutes or till twists are warm. Makes 24 twists.

Greek-Style Pastries

The spinach, feta cheese, and phyllo dough make them Greek. All of the ingredients together make them great!

　6　cups torn spinach
　　　　(8 ounces)
　2　3-ounce packages cream
　　　　cheese, softened
　½　cup crumbled feta cheese
　¼　cup grated Parmesan cheese
　　　Dash pepper
　15　sheets frozen phyllo dough
　　　　(18x14-inch rectangles),
　　　　thawed
　⅔　cup butter *or* margarine,
　　　　melted

● For filling, rinse spinach in cool water. In a large saucepan cook spinach, covered, in just the water that clings to the spinach. Reduce heat when steam forms; cook, covered, about 3 minutes or till tender. Drain well. In a small mixing bowl stir together cream cheese, feta cheese, Parmesan cheese, and pepper. Stir in spinach; set aside.

● Unfold phyllo dough; cover with a damp towel or clear plastic wrap. Spread 1 sheet of phyllo dough flat. Brush with some of the melted butter or margarine. Top with another sheet of phyllo dough. Brush with more butter or margarine. Add another sheet, making a total of 3 sheets of phyllo dough; brush with butter or margarine.

● Cut the stack, crosswise, into 2-inch strips. Place 1 rounded teaspoon of filling near the end of each strip of phyllo. Starting at the end, fold the dough repeatedly over the filling, forming a triangle that encloses the filling.

● Repeat with remaining dough and filling. Brush the tops of each triangle with the remaining butter or margarine. Transfer to a freezer container or bags. Seal, label, and freeze.

● **To serve,** arrange frozen pastries on an ungreased baking sheet. Bake in a 375° oven for 15 to 20 minutes or till puffed and brown. Serve warm or cool. Makes 45 pastries.

1 Stacking and cutting the phyllo dough

Use a pastry brush to spread one sheet of phyllo dough with some of the melted butter or margarine. Top with another sheet of phyllo dough. Brush with more butter. Add another sheet of phyllo dough, making a total of three sheets; brush with butter. With a sharp knife, cut the stack of buttered phyllo dough, crosswise, into 2-inch strips.

Remember: Keep the unused sheets of phyllo dough covered with a damp towel or clear plastic wrap. The dough is fragile and dries out easily if not covered.

2 Folding the pastries

To assemble pastries, place one rounded teaspoon of filling mixture near the end of each strip of phyllo dough. Fold the end over the filling at a 45-degree angle. Continue folding to form a triangle that encloses the filling, using the entire three-layer strip of phyllo dough.

Index

Index